P9-CRQ-663

rule

your

day

**6 Keys to Maximizing Your Success
and Accelerating Your Dreams**

JOEL OSTEEN

Faith
Words

New York   Nashville

ALSO BY JOEL OSTEEN

A Fresh New Day Journal

All Things Are Working for
Your Good
*Daily Readings from All Things Are
Working for Your Good*

Blessed in the Darkness
Blessed in the Darkness Journal
Blessed in the Darkness Study Guide

Break Out!
Break Out! Journal
Daily Readings from Break Out!

Empty Out the Negative

Every Day a Friday
Every Day a Friday Journal
*Daily Readings from Every
Day a Friday*

Fresh Start
Fresh Start Study Guide

I Declare
I Declare Personal Application Guide

Next Level Thinking
Next Level Thinking Journal
Next Level Thinking Study Guide
*Daily Readings from Next Level
Thinking*

Peaceful on Purpose
Peaceful on Purpose Study Guide
Peace for the Season

The Abundance Mind-set

The Power of Favor
The Power of Favor Study Guide

The Power of I Am
The Power of I Am Journal
The Power of I Am Study Guide
Daily Readings from The Power of I Am

Think Better, Live Better
Think Better, Live Better Journal
Think Better, Live Better Study Guide
*Daily Readings from Think Better,
Live Better*

Two Words That Will
Change Your Life Today

With Victoria Osteen
Our Best Life Together
Wake Up to Hope Devotional

You Are Stronger than You Think
*You Are Stronger than You Think
Study Guide*

You Can, You Will
You Can, You Will Journal
Daily Readings from You Can, You Will

Your Best Life Now
Your Best Life Begins Each Morning
Your Best Life Now for Moms
Your Best Life Now Journal
Your Best Life Now Study Guide
Daily Readings from Your Best Life Now
*Scriptures and Meditations for
Your Best Life Now*
Starting Your Best Life Now

rule

your

day

Cover design by Faceout Studios
Cover photography by Shutterstock
Cover copyright © 2022 by Hachette Book Group, Inc.

FaithWords
Hachette Book Group
1290 Avenue of the Americas, New York, NY 10104
faithwords.com
twitter.com/faithwords

First Edition: March 2022

FaithWords is a division of Hachette Book Group, Inc. The FaithWords name and logo are trademarks of Hachette Book Group, Inc.

The publisher is not responsible for websites (or their content) that are not owned by the publisher.

The Hachette Speakers Bureau provides a wide range of authors for speaking events. To find out more, go to www.hachettespeakersbureau.com or call (866) 376-6591.

Library of Congress Cataloging-in-Publication Data

Names: Osteen, Joel, author.
Title: Rule your day : 6 keys to maximizing your success and accelerating your dreams / Joel Osteen.
Description: First edition. | New York : FaithWords, [2022]
Identifiers: LCCN 2021041423 | ISBN 9781546041856 (hardcover) | ISBN 9781546041825 (large print) | ISBN 9781546041832 (ebook)
Subjects: LCSH: Success—Religious aspects—Christianity. | Control (Psychology)—Religious aspects—Christianity.
Classification: LCC BV4598.3 .O79 2022 | DDC 158—dc23
LC record available at https://lccn.loc.gov/2021041423

ISBN: 9781546041856 (hardcover), 9781546041832 (ebook), 9781546041825 (large print), 9781546002284 (international trade paperback)

Printed in the United States of America

LSC-H

Printing 1, 2021

CONTENTS

CHAPTER ONE

Rule Your Day

You have a space that belongs only to you. It's your thoughts, your attitudes, and your emotions. It's who you spend time with. It's what you watch and listen to. That's your atmosphere. That's what you have control over. The reason some people live worried, offended, and negative is because they let everything in. They listen to the news all day, they dwell on the medical report, and they go to lunch with people who are critical. Somebody cuts them off in traffic, and that sours the rest of their morning. The problem is that they're not ruling their atmosphere. You have to be careful what you allow in. You can't stop every negative thing from coming, but you can stop it from getting down in your spirit.

You need to keep your atmosphere full of faith,

full of praise, full of hope, full of victory. It's up to you to say to anything that tries to poison that atmosphere, "No, thanks. You're not welcome here." If somebody leaves you out at work and doesn't invite you to a meeting, the offense will come, saying, "Be angry, be bitter. That's not right." You can let that offense in and live upset, or you can say, "Sorry, offense. You're not welcome here. Sorry, bitterness. There's no place for you. I'm going to stay in peace. I'm going to enjoy this day." You don't have control over what other people do, but you have control over your thoughts, your attitudes, and how you respond.

The writer of Proverbs says, "A person who doesn't rule his spirit is like a city with broken down walls." In King Solomon's time, the walls were what protected the city. If the walls were down, the opposition could come in and take the city. In the same way, if you don't keep some walls up around your spirit, if you don't rule your atmosphere and put up some boundaries, then everything is going to get in. If your child is off course, instead of trusting that God has him in the palms of His hands, worry will get in and you won't be able to sleep at night. If your business slows down or you lose a client, instead of knowing that God is your source and that He's going to provide, stress will come and anxious thoughts will say, *What am I going to do?* If someone is talking about you, trying to make you look bad, instead of letting God fight your battles, you will let the offense in. You'll live defensive, trying to prove to them that you're okay, which is wasting valuable time on what doesn't matter. You don't need their approval; God has already approved you. Now keep your walls up. Quit allowing all that negativity into your spirit. Your time is too valuable, your assignment too important, to let everything in. Be

> *If you don't keep some walls up around your spirit, if you don't rule your atmosphere and put up some boundaries, then everything is going to get in.*

selective. If it's not positive, hopeful, and of a good report, don't dwell on it. You can't control the whole world, but you can control your atmosphere.

Rule over Your Kingdom

The Scripture says that God has made you to be a king, that you are to reign in life. Negative things will come, but you have to remember that you're the ruler. You have the authority to decide what you allow in. *Am I going to dwell on this offense? Am I going to hang around this person who's pulling me down? Am I going to stay focused on this bad break and live in self-pity?* It's up to you. You rule over your kingdom with your attitudes and with what you choose to focus on.

When we turn on the news, there's so much that's negative. We hear about natural disasters, the divisiveness in politics, the unrest in our society. If you allow that division to get into your spirit, if you allow the disrespect and the anger to get in, it's going to pollute your thoughts, steal your joy, and make you sour. You have to be proactive. What are you watching and what are you listening to? Is it building you up, making you more positive and more hopeful, or is it tearing you down, stressing you out, making you angry and upset? You don't need that in your atmosphere. Life is hard enough without adding all these negative things that make it more difficult.

> What are you watching and what are you listening to?

A man told me that as he drove to work he listened to talk radio for an hour every day. It was about news and politics, with people calling in to argue and debate. He would get so riled up, so upset, that by the time he got to work he was angry and on edge. He said, "Joel, I didn't like who I had become. Nobody wanted to be around me. I was so hard to get along with." One day he happened to come across our SiriusXM station and started to listen. Instead of putting in all the negativity that was contaminating him hour after hour, he started putting in uplifting words of faith, hope, and victory. He said, "I'm a different person now. I'm positive. I'm grateful. I look forward to work. I enjoy the other people." His coworker even asked him what happened to him, why he was so much happier and friendlier. It was because he got rid of the poison in his atmosphere.

I like to watch the news, and it's good to stay informed, but you can't listen to the news for hours a day and stay in faith. You can't take that into your spirit and have the energy, the focus, and the creativity to be your best. "Well, Joel, I wish God would help me do better." God has done His part. He made you a king. He's given you the authority and the power to rule

> *You can't control all that's around you, but you can control what gets in you.*

your atmosphere. You can't control all that's around you, but you can control what gets in you. Are your walls up? Are you ruling your spirit?

Who Are You Sitting With?

It's also important who you're spending time with. Evaluate your friendships. Are your friends making you better, inspiring you, and challenging you to go further? Or are they pulling you down, causing you to compromise, and bringing out the worst in you? That's contaminating your atmosphere. You're going to become like the people you hang around. If your friends don't have what you want, if they're not rising to new levels, if they don't have good attitudes, if they're not faithful and trustworthy, you need to make a change. Life is short, and you don't have time to waste with people who are not adding to your life. Yes, we need to help others come up higher, but you need a few friends who help you come up higher. This is one of the main things

Spirits are transferable.

that holds people back. If you stop spending time with the wrong people, your life will go to a new level. You shouldn't go to lunch with people from the office who are jealous, who talk about the boss, who complain about the company. Spirits are transferable. If you hang around jealous people, you're going to become jealous. If you hang around unfaithful people, you're going to become unfaithful.

The Scripture says, "Don't sit inactive in the path of the ungodly." That means you can't be passive when it comes to people polluting your life. "Joel, I've been friends with them for years. If I don't eat lunch with them, they may get their feelings hurt." What if you miss your destiny? What if they keep you from the awesome future God has in store? Don't sit inactive and let them poison your atmosphere. Your ears are not garbage cans to hear gossip. You weren't created to take in the latest rumors. You have greatness in you. God has called you to leave your mark, to take your family to a new level. Don't waste your valuable time on petty things, with small-minded people who are not moving you forward.

The less time you spend with some people the better off you're going to be. Some people are dream stealers. They'll tell you all the reasons why you can't accomplish your goal, or why you can't get well, or

> *Some people are dream stealers.*

how you'll never break the addiction. You don't need that poison in your atmosphere. Don't sit inactive with people who don't believe in you, with people who don't come into agreement with your dream.

You Need Some Eagles

When we were trying to acquire the Compaq Center, we first met with a group of attorneys. One of those attorneys said, "Joel, I'll help you, but I don't think you'll get it. It's too big a battle. The city is not going to sell it to a church." That went in one ear and out the other. He might as well have been talking to the wall. I thought, *Sorry, doubt. You're not welcome here. Sorry, limited thinking. You don't belong in this atmosphere. You don't know who my God is. I'm staying full of faith, full of hope, full of expectancy.* After we left that meeting, I told our staff that I didn't want that man on our team. He was experienced, respected, and knowledgeable, but if someone is not for you, if you have to talk them into what God put in your heart, you don't need them. Don't let them poison your spirit and convince you that you can't accomplish your dream. Rule your atmosphere.

Get rid of the naysayers. Quit spending time with people who don't see your greatness, who don't value what you have to offer, and who don't recognize the calling on your life. I've learned that if you get rid of the wrong people, God will bring you the right people. He'll bring divine connections, people who will come into agreement with you, people who will thrust you forward and help you reach your destiny.

The only thing that's holding some people back is who they're spending time with. Life is too short for you to spend with negative, can't-do-it, jealous, critical, small-minded people. You need some eagles in your life. You need some people who soar, people who are doing great things, people who have a great attitude. But here's the key: You can't soar with the eagles if you're hanging around with the chickens. Chickens are people who have their heads down, focused on the ground, focused on what they can't do. "This problem is too big." You can't reach new levels hanging out with turkeys, with people who compromise, who take the easy way out, who are mediocre. You won't see your greatness hanging around with crows, with people who complain,

> *You can't soar with the eagles if you're hanging around with the chickens.*

who find fault, who always see the worst. You're an eagle. God created you to soar. Now you need to associate with other eagles, with people who inspire you to rise higher, not with people who drag you down.

When you're around certain people, they drain all your energy. They're always having a problem, telling you what's wrong and how bad life is. They're energy suckers. When you leave them, you feel as though you just ran a marathon. You can't take that in on a regular basis and reach your potential. Yes, it's fine to help and to encourage them, but if you're doing all the giving and never receiving, that's out of balance. You need someone who encourages you, someone who speaks life into you. Don't sit inactive around people who you know are limiting you, who are not bringing the best out of you. "Joel, if I don't hang around them, I won't have any friends. I'll be lonely." You may be lonely for a season, but God will bring you new friends, better friends, friends who push you up and do not tear you down.

Rule Your Atmosphere

In Psalm 59, David was on the run from King Saul, hiding in the desert. He had been good to Saul, but

Saul was jealous of him. Saul couldn't stand people celebrating David more than him. Saul and his army were tracking David down, making his life miserable. David said, "I have done them no wrong, but they have set an ambush for me. They come at me at night, snarling like vicious dogs." David went on and on describing how bad it was. He could have been panicked and gotten upset. But in the middle of all this turmoil, David went on to say to God, "But as for me, I will sing about Your power. I will shout for joy each morning. For You are my refuge, a place of safety in my time of distress." David understood this principle. He couldn't control Saul. He couldn't make Saul not be jealous. He couldn't change the minds of his enemies, but he could rule his atmosphere. He didn't let the worry in, the fear in, the bitterness in, the panic in. His attitude was, *I'm going to stay in peace. I'm not going to think about how unfair it is. I'm not going to dwell on what didn't work out. God, I'm going to praise You in the middle of this storm. I'm going to shout for joy despite what's coming against me.* You can't rule other people's atmosphere, and you can't make them do what's right, but you can rule your atmosphere.

The Scripture says, "Hold your peace, remain at

rest, and God will fight your battles." You may be in a situation that's unfair—somebody did you wrong, you're dealing with an illness, you went through a loss. You could be worried, bitter, and upset. You can't control what happened, and you can't make that go away. This is where you have to dig down deep as David did and say, "I'm keeping my walls up. I'm not letting that negative into my spirit. I'm going to keep singing praises. I'm going to keep thanking God. I'm going to keep speaking the victory." When you remain at rest, God will fight your battles. He'll take care of your enemies. He'll pay you back for the unfair things. He'll bring beauty out of those ashes. Don't be controlled by what you don't have control over. You can't stop the Sauls from coming after you. You can't stop people from being jealous. You can't stop the bad breaks. What you can control is what you allow in.

> *Don't be controlled by what you don't have control over.*

A lady told me about how opinionated one of her husband's relatives was. Soon after this couple had been married, this relative started making cutting, demeaning remarks about her viewpoints. Every time they were at a family get-together, this man would say something that offended her. She would get upset, and it would ruin their whole trip. Just like clockwork, it happened time and time again. She got to the place where she dreaded going to their family events. Finally, she told her husband, "You have to do something about that man. He's your relative." She expected him to say, "You're right. Nobody should talk to you like that. I'm going to set him straight." But the husband said, "I love you, but I can't control him. He has every right to have his opinion. He can say what he wants to say, but you have every right to not let it offend you." He was saying, "You have to rule your atmosphere. You have to put your walls up. You can't keep the offenses from coming, but you can keep them from getting in."

That day was a turning point for this lady. The relative didn't change, but she changed. She quit letting him upset her. When you allow other people to contaminate your atmosphere, you're giving away your power. You're letting them control you. Sometimes we're waiting for the circumstances to change. "When this financial crisis is over, I'll quit being so stressed." "When my boss treats me better, I'll quit dreading going to work." "When I get through this illness, I'll quit being so worried." No, start ruling your

> *When you allow other people to contaminate your atmosphere, you're giving away your power.*

atmosphere. You have the authority to allow in only what you want in. You don't have to let the offense in, the worry, the self-pity. Quit dwelling on it. When it comes up in your mind, turn it around and say, "Father, thank You that You're fighting my battles. Thank You that Your being for me is more than the world being against me."

Power to Remain Calm

The Scripture says, "God has given you the power to remain calm in times of adversity." When trouble comes, you don't have to get upset. When your plans don't work out, you don't have to fall apart. When someone is rude, you don't have to get offended. You have the power to remain calm. It's because you're a king. God has given you the authority to rule over your kingdom—over your mind, your attitude, and your response. You can't rule over someone else. You can't rule over all your circumstances. That's not up to you. That's in God's hands. You control what you can control, and you have to trust God to take care of what you can't control.

In 2003, the Houston City Council voted for us to have the Compaq Center for our facility. It had been a two-year battle. We had worked hard, convinced different council members, and God caused it to all fall into place. It was a great victory. The vote was on a Wednesday, and that night we had a big celebration at the church. The next day, Victoria and I and our children went out of town to take a few days off. We were on cloud nine, so excited. After we arrived at the hotel and started unpacking, my brother-in-law Kevin, our church administrator, called and said, "Joel, a large company just filed a federal lawsuit to try to keep us from moving into the Compaq Center. They say we are in violation of the deed restrictions." I asked him what that meant. He said, "It means we can't move in because it's in the legal system, and it could take years to work out." The attorneys said there was no guarantee that we would win. This was less than twenty-four hours after one of the greatest victories of our lives.

Victoria overheard the whole conversation. She stopped unpacking and said, "Joel, what are you going to do?" I said, "I'm going down to the beach." She asked, "What are you going to do there?" I responded, "I'm going to swim." She looked me in the eyes and said, "Aren't you worried?" I answered, "No, we did our part; now it's in God's hands. I'm not going to worry about something that I can't change. I'm going to stay at rest, and I'm going to trust God to fight my battles." Yes, worry came, disappointment came, and frustration came, but I kept my walls up. I didn't allow that in my atmosphere.

When you've had a setback, when you're facing difficulties, that's a very important time. The enemy is going to bombard your space—your mind, your emotions—and even use other people to try to discourage you and get you worried and full of doubt. "Why did this happen?" That's when you have to take your authority and say, "No, I am not allowing that in my atmosphere. I'm not dwelling on it. I'm not reliving my hurts. I'm not thinking about what didn't work out. I'm staying in faith. I know that God is still on the throne. I know that He didn't bring me this

> *If you do your part and control what you can control, if you rule your atmosphere, your thoughts, and your attitudes, then God will do His part.*

far to leave me. I know that the enemy wouldn't be trying to stop me if there wasn't something awesome in my future." If you do your part and control what you can control, if you rule your atmosphere, your thoughts, and your attitudes, then God will do His part. He'll make things happen that you couldn't make happen.

Rule the Day

There's a juice bar franchise that has as its motto: "Rule the Day." They encourage you to eat the right foods and take the right vitamins so you can have a healthy day. I like that phrase, *Rule the Day*. When you get up in the morning, make the decision: "I'm going to rule my thoughts today. I'm not just going to think about whatever comes to mind. I'm going to think thoughts that are positive, hopeful, and encouraging, on purpose. I'm not going to spend time with just anyone today. I'm going to rule my day and be selective. I'm going to associate with eagles. I'm going to rule my attitude today. I'm going to see the best, I'm going to be grateful, and I'm going to stay in peace. I'm going to rule my emotions today. I'm going to forgive the wrongs, I'm going to overlook insults, and I'm going to give people the benefit of the doubt." Before you leave the house in the morning, it's important to make this decision that nothing that happens is going to upset you. You're going to stay in peace. Then when difficulties come—traffic is bad, your boss is rude, your child has a problem—you've already decided you're going to rule your day. You have your walls up. You're not going to live upset.

We should go out every day expecting the best, but knowing that everything may not be perfect. There may be delays, interruptions, and people who are hard to deal with. Don't let that ruin your day. Rule your day. Keep the negative out of your atmosphere. God is directing your steps. Whatever happens is not a surprise to Him. He's given you the power to remain calm in times of adversity. God never promised that you would have the power to avoid adversity, or to not have challenges, or to have a perfect day. The fact is that every day can be a good day if you rule your atmosphere. David had a good day even when Saul was chasing him. I had a good day at the beach when that company filed a lawsuit. Quit waiting for all the circumstances to be perfect. You can have a good day in the middle of a crisis. You can have a good day even though you have challenges at

> *Keep the negative out of your atmosphere.*

work, even though you're dealing with an illness, even though some people don't like you. Stay calm, stay in faith, and rule your day. Make the decision as David did and say, "This is the day the Lord has made. I'm going to live it in faith. I'm going to be happy today. I'm going to be good to others. I'm going to make the most of this day."

One evening I called to order a pizza, which I have done for many years. The first thing they always ask for is your phone number. When a young lady answered the phone, I said hello very politely and started to give her my number. You would have thought I had just committed a major crime. She practically screamed in my ear, "Sir, I am not ready for your phone number! When I want your phone number, I will ask you for your phone number!" At that moment, I suddenly didn't feel like a pastor. I felt some other things rising up. I had to make a decision: *Am I going to rule my atmosphere, or am I going to let her poison my atmosphere? Am I going to keep my*

> *People are always trying to bring their atmosphere into your atmosphere.*

walls up, or am I going to be offended? People are always trying to bring their atmosphere into your atmosphere. People who are hurting, who have issues and are dealing with things, will try to put their poison on you. They're not bad people; they're just hurting. The mistake we make too often is to take the bait. We let the offense in, get upset, and do to them what they did to us. But you don't overcome evil with more evil; you overcome evil with good. I thought to myself, *I've already made the decision that I'm going to stay in peace today. I'm not going to get upset. I'm going to rule this day.*

You've heard the phrase *Kill them with kindness.* That's what I decided to do. I thought of anything that I could possibly compliment her on. God knows that I had to use my imagination. I said, "I sure appreciate you answering the phone so quickly and taking my order, being so efficient. You guys always make the best pizzas, and you're always on time." I went on and on lying...I mean encouraging. By the time I was finished, she was throwing in hot wings, sodas, and coupons. She was my best friend.

Be Calm, Cool, and Steady

The apostle Paul told Timothy, "As for you, be calm, cool, and steady." Some people let things upset them way too easily, whether it's the traffic, the weather, or a grumpy clerk. I wonder how much more you would enjoy life and how much higher you would go if you start ruling the day. Keep your walls up. Don't let everything get in your spirit. You can't stop the negative from coming, but you can keep it from getting down in you. You're a king. You have a kingdom. You're in charge of your thoughts and your attitude. Start ruling your atmosphere. At the beginning of the day, make the decision that you're going to stay in peace. You're not going to let things upset you. You're going to be calm, cool, and steady. If you do this, I believe and declare that you're not only going to enjoy your life more, but you're going to see more of God's favor. He's going to fight your battles and take care of what's trying to stop you. You're going to rise higher, overcome obstacles, and see new levels of your destiny.

CHAPTER TWO

Daily Direction

God says in Psalm 32, "I will lead you down the best path for your life." He has the wisdom, the guidance, and the direction we need, but it's not going to happen automatically. There's something we have to do. Every morning we have to go to Him and say, "God, I'm ready for my assignment. Show me what to do, show me where to go, give me the words to speak, make the path clear." Asking for wisdom, guidance, and instruction is an act of surrender. It takes humility to say, "God, You know what's best for me. I need Your help. I can't do this on my own. Open the right doors, close the wrong doors. Show me the best path."

The Scripture says that when you acknowledge God in all your ways, He will direct your path. Too often we make our plans without consulting God, then we ask Him to bless them. We wonder why it's a struggle, why it feels like it's always uphill. We have it backward. We're making the move, then asking God for His help. The right way is to ask God first. "God, is this what You want me to do? Should I date this person? Should I start this project? Should I take this trip? Should I make this purchase?" If you feel peace about it, go forward. If not, hold off. God knows what's best for us.

In the Lord's Prayer, Jesus says, "Give us this day our daily bread." He didn't say "our weekly bread" or "our monthly bread." It's not enough to think, *Joel, I go to church every Sunday.* Every morning you need to go to God for your daily bread, your daily wisdom, your daily direction. Too many times we're trying to do things only in our own strength, our own intellect, our own ability. That's going to limit you. God knows things you don't know. He sees things you can't see. He knows the right people who should be in your life. He knows where the danger is and where the

> *In the Lord's Prayer, Jesus says, "Give us this day our daily bread." He didn't say "our weekly bread" or "our monthly bread."*

dead ends are. God knows how to catapult you years ahead. He knows how to thrust you into your destiny. You have an advantage.

Are you taking time to get your daily bread? Sometimes we rush out of the house in the morning, saying, "I'm in a hurry. I don't have time. I have to get to work." I live by this saying: "Don't ever meet with people before you meet with God." If you take time to acknowledge God and say, "God, I need You today. Lead me, guide me. Keep me on the right path," not only will your day go better, but God will keep you from making major mistakes.

> *"Don't ever meet with people before you meet with God."*

Daily Wisdom Has Your Name on It

A few years before my father went to be with the Lord in 1999, Victoria and I came across a construction permit for the last full power commercial television station in Houston. After having spent years behind the scenes at Lakewood doing the television production, I was so excited about being able to put this station on the air. We were building it from the ground up. We had to find a place for the tower, buy the programming, and hire the staff. While it was very exciting, I wasn't experienced in broadcast television. I knew production, but this was beyond my expertise. Every morning I would do what I'm asking you to do and start my day off saying, "God, I can't do this in my own strength, my own ability. I need Your help. Lord, lead me to the right people, guide me down the best path, and keep me from making a mistake." What was I doing? Getting my daily bread, my daily instruction.

One day we were about to purchase the most expensive piece of equipment for the station, which was going to cost a couple of million dollars. Our engineers had researched it and come up with their recommendation of the make and model. I didn't know anything about it; they were the experts. It was a leading brand. But a couple of days before we put the purchase order in, a friend of mine called out of the blue. I hadn't talked to him in a long time. He called about something unrelated to the station, and we talked about fifteen minutes. Right before he hung up, he made a comment about the manufacturer of the piece of equipment we were going to buy. He said in passing that he had heard that the company was struggling, and it looked as though they could go out of business. He made the statement, "I feel bad for people who have their equipment." He didn't have any idea we were about to place an order with that company. When he said that, chills went up and down my spine. He didn't know it, but God was speaking through him. I hung up and called our engineers. They researched it and found out it was true. If he had called a few days later, it would have been too late. We would have been stuck with equipment that was soon obsolete, not supported, and a big headache.

Some people think that phone call was a coincidence, but I know it was God directing my path. That's what happens when you get your daily bread, when every morning you ask God for wisdom. You're showing your dependence on Him. When you humble yourself like that, the Scripture says that God will exalt you. A lot of people are too prideful. They think, *I don't need anybody's help. I can do this on my own. Look how successful I am already, Joel.* Yes, but think about where you could be if you would start to acknowledge God. Think about

> *Don't do it on your own. That's going to limit you.*

the mistakes and heartache He could have saved you from. Think of the dead ends you could have avoided. Think about the favor, the opportunities, and the doors you couldn't open but God will open. Don't do it on your own. That's going to limit you. Start getting your daily bread, your daily wisdom, your daily direction. It's available; it has your name on it. Take time each morning to acknowledge God.

What Worked Yesterday May Not Work Today

When the Israelites were in the desert headed toward the Promised Land, God gave them manna to eat each morning. It was something like bread that formed on the ground. The manna would last only for one day. Every morning they had to go out and get a new supply. I'm sure some people thought, *I'm going to gather up enough for a whole week. I don't want to come tomorrow. I'll save time and energy and get it all done at once.* But they woke up the next day and all the manna was spoiled. They couldn't eat it. The principle was that every morning you had to go out and get fresh manna. The word *manna* in Hebrew is translated "What is it?" When we go to God each day for that fresh manna, the right attitude is, *God, what is it that You want me to do? What is my assignment? What is the right path?* It is not giving God all of our orders, telling Him what to do, and how to do it. Rather, it is saying, "God, I'm ready. Show me the path, show me how to overcome this challenge, show me how to accomplish my dreams. Give me Your ideas, Your wisdom, and Your direction."

Are you getting your daily manna? Are you checking in with headquarters to get your assignment each morning, asking God, "What is it?" Or are you on autopilot, just doing what you've always done? The challenge with that approach is that what worked in the past may not work today. Sometimes God will do things a different way. In Exodus 17, when the Israelites were thirsty in the wilderness, they needed water. God told Moses to strike the rock at Horeb, and when he did, water flowed out freely. He was so thankful. It was a great miracle. Later, in Numbers 20, when the people were thirsty again and there was no water, God told Moses to speak to the rock at Kadesh. The problem was that Moses was on autopilot, and he was so angry with the people who were complaining against God that he didn't listen to God's directions.

He thought, *Same problem, same desert, and a similar rock. I've got this down. I don't need daily direction. I've already overcome this challenge once. I can do it again.* Moses was so upset that he struck the rock twice and water gushed out for the Israelites and their livestock. But it came at a great cost for Moses. The Lord said that because Moses did not listen and honor Him before the people, because he did not do it His way, he could not enter the Promised Land.

If Moses had listened, he would have heard God saying, "Moses, I have water for you, but it's not going to happen the way it happened at Horeb." The principle is that you can't live off yesterday's bread and expect to have victory today. Yesterday's information may not work today. God is a God of freshness. He likes to do new things. It's easy to get stuck in a rut thinking, *I don't need daily bread. I don't need to listen. I've overcome this challenge in the past, and I'm going to use the same tactics to overcome it this time.* But as with Moses, sometimes the old way is the wrong way. You need some fresh manna. If not, you'll strike the rock when you're supposed to speak to the rock. It's a simple tweak, but you'll only hear it if you're getting your daily bread.

> God is a God of freshness. He likes to do new things.

Stay open for change. Be willing to try something new. What made you successful five years ago may not make you successful today. What worked in your marriage in the past may not work today. Why don't you get some fresh manna? Have the attitude, *God, I'm open for new things.* I've heard it said that if you don't innovate you will evaporate. You can't rely on what got you to where you are to keep you where you are. Things are changing. Somebody wants your job, somebody wants your spouse, somebody wants your dream. The world is moving forward. You can't afford to stay on autopilot, to just coast and do things the same way. You'll get left behind. The good news is that God has daily favor, daily wisdom, daily ideas, daily abundance. If you stay open, He'll lead you into the fullness of your destiny.

> *You can't rely on what got you to where you are to keep you where you are.*

Listen to What God Is Saying Now

Why couldn't Moses just strike the rock again? It worked the first time. It seems as though it would make more sense to just let it happen the same way. It's because God wants us to rely on Him, not some formula. "If I do this and do that and do this other, God will promote me." If that's all it took, we wouldn't need God. "Just follow these steps to success. Just strike the rock all the time." That's not faith; that's more like magic. God changes the method on purpose so we have to come to Him for our daily bread. He's looking for people who recognize that He is the source of our strength, the source of our success, and that in Him is health, freedom, abundance, ideas, and creativity. When you rely on Him, He'll take you from victory to victory, but here's the key: He may not do it the same way. Could it be that you're stuck, not seeing

> *Could it be that you're stuck, not seeing promotion, because like Moses you're still striking the rock when God is telling you to speak to the rock?*

promotion, because like Moses you're still striking the rock when God is telling you to speak to the rock? You're stuck in tradition, in how it happened in the past, trying to duplicate the same thing, when God is wanting to do a new thing in a new way, with new ideas and new people, and bring new talents out of you. If you start getting your daily bread, listening to what God is saying now, following that still small voice, then you will see water begin to flow in greater ways.

David understood this principle. In 2 Samuel 5, he had just been made king over Israel. When the Philistines heard about it, they came in full force to the Valley of Rephaim to attack him. David was a warrior who had conquered many enemies. He loved a good battle. Now he was the king. I'm sure David was on a high, thinking these people had picked the wrong man to fight. They were in for trouble. His nature was to attack. He could have thought that there was nothing to pray about, that this was an easy decision. He had won hundreds of battles. What was one more? But here's why David was a man after God's own heart. The Scripture says, "David inquired of the Lord, 'Shall I go attack the Philistines? Will You hand them over to me?'" Notice his humility. He didn't say, "I've got this, no problem. Been there, done that." He took time to inquire of the Lord. Before he went to battle, he got quiet and said, "God, what should I do?" He was getting his daily direction. He didn't assume that because something had worked in the past it would work in the future.

David asked a very significant question: "God, will You hand this enemy over to me?" It seems like that would have been a given. God had just put him in charge of the Israelites, His chosen people. Surely God wouldn't let him be defeated. But the fact is, we're not supposed to fight every battle. David was wise enough to ask, "Am I supposed to attack?" He was saying, "God, I don't want to go if You're not going with me." He was showing his dependence on God. He recognized where his strength, his favor, and his ability came from.

> *We've all fought battles where we didn't come out as we thought we would. Maybe it was because we didn't inquire of the Lord.*

Sometimes we assume that if there's an obstacle, something's trying to stop us, there's no question that we get in there and go to battle. God is on our side. But the wise approach is to say, "God, what is Your plan? What is it that You want me to do with this opposition? Shall I attack, or shall I be still and let You fight for me? If I go in, will You give me the victory?" We've all fought battles where we didn't come out as we thought we would. Maybe it was because we didn't inquire of the Lord. David didn't rely on his strength, his experience, his talent, or his connections. He knew there was something more important than all of that. Without God's blessing, he wouldn't be successful.

The Scripture goes on to say, "The Lord said to David, 'Go, for I will surely hand the Philistines over to you.'" Once David got clear direction, once he knew that he had God's blessing, he went out and defeated the Philistines. If we would do as David did and inquire of the Lord before we get into conflict, before we make big decisions, and go to God for fresh manna, for daily direction, it would save us a lot of heartache and pain. I've learned what God orders He will pay for. But God is not obligated to bring victory to battles we're not supposed to be in. Yes, God is merciful, and He'll help us, but it's much better to inquire of the Lord before you make an important decision. Don't just assume that because it happened last time, it's going to happen the same way this time.

> *I've learned what God orders He will pay for. But God is not obligated to bring victory to battles we're not supposed to be in.*

A few months later, the Philistines came back to

the same valley to attack David again. David could have thought, *This is a no-brainer. There's no need to ask God this time. I know what to do, just get in there and defeat them.* But David realized he couldn't rely on yesterday's manna. He knew yesterday's information might not be appropriate for today's challenge. The Scripture says, "David inquired of the Lord again, and the Lord said, 'Do not attack them.'" It was the same enemy and the same valley, but this time God said, "I'm going to do it another way. I don't want you to attack them from the front. I want you to circle around them." He told David, "When you hear the rustling of the mulberry trees, that will be a sign that I've gone before you and defeated your enemy. Then you can go in at once." If David had not inquired of the Lord, he would have done it as he did the first way, assuming it worked last time. Common sense was telling him that surely it would work this time. But God's ways are not our ways. He doesn't want you to get hooked on a formula; He wants you to be hooked on Him. You have to

> *God's ways are not our ways. He doesn't want you to get hooked on a formula; He wants you to be hooked on Him.*

develop this habit of getting daily direction, fresh manna, by asking, "God, how do You want me to respond to this problem? How do I deal with this situation in my finances or in my health? God, give me Your wisdom, Your ideas, Your favor." That's how God leads you down the best path for your life. You can't respond to every problem the same way.

Only Fight the Battles That Are Yours to Fight

When I was in my early twenties, there was a couple that I really liked, and I went overboard to be good to them. They were friendly to me, but it always seemed as though I wasn't doing enough for them. My nature was to do more and make sure they knew I appreciated them. So I did more favors for them and went out of my way to be nice. Several years later, when they moved to another state, I gave them money to help with the moving costs and helped them pack up. I knew down inside that's what I was supposed to be doing. I was taking the high road, going the extra mile, and I felt good about it. I believe that God continued to bless me for it. A few years after they moved, I heard from a friend that this couple was upset with me, thinking I should have helped them more, and on and on. Here I had helped them more than anyone. That bothered me because back then I wanted everyone to like me. My nature was to do more, to get in there and fix it, to go the extra mile.

When I prayed about this situation, when I asked God for fresh manna, deep down inside I heard something say strongly, "Joel, leave them alone. No matter what you do, they're not going to be for you." It was the same battle and the same people, but a different approach. If I hadn't learned to get daily direction as I'm telling you to do, I'd still be frustrated, trying to convince somebody to like me who was never going to like me.

Are you fighting a battle that you're not supposed to fight? If God's not giving you the permission, you're going to do it in your own strength, your own ability. It will be a constant struggle; there's no grace for it. Just because it was right in the past doesn't mean it's right for today. You need to get daily direction. Like David, you may be skilled in battle, you're tough, and you can take on the best of them. But you have to check in with headquarters and get your assignment. "God, am I supposed to fight this battle? Show me how to overcome. Show me the right steps to take." Then listen to what you're feeling down inside—not in

> *Just because it was right in the past doesn't mean it's right for today.*

your mind but in your heart. Listen to the still small voice. It's a knowing, an impression. You can't explain it, but you just know this is what you're supposed to do. That's God giving you daily wisdom. That's what's going to lead you down the best path.

Be Wise and Always Consult the Lord

This is where Joshua and the Israelites got off course. In Joshua 9, they had entered the Promised Land and just seen the walls of Jericho come down, which was a great victory. They had defeated other armies along the way. God's favor was on them. But there was a group of people called the Gibeonites who lived in neighboring cities where the Israelites had camped. When they had heard how powerful and successful the Israelites were, they knew they couldn't compete with them and that they were going to be driven out of their cities as well. So they came up with a plan to try to deceive Joshua. They loaded their donkeys with old worn-out sacks. They put on old clothes that had holes in them and sandals that were falling apart. Their wineskins were cracked and mended. They had bread that they had left out on purpose so it would be old, stale, and crusty. They did this so it would look as though they had traveled a long distance. They showed up at Joshua's camp and said, "Joshua, we've come from a far, far land. We've traveled for months and months. We're tired, and we're hungry. Please make a peace treaty with us. Let us live here, and we'll work for you."

Joshua asked, "How do I know that you're not from one of the neighboring cities that I'm about to conquer? How can I be sure you don't live close by?" They said, "Joshua, look at this bread. It was fresh when we left, but now it's old and moldy. Our wineskins were new, but now they're cracked and falling apart. And look at our clothes. They were dry-cleaned before we left. This shirt had starch in it, but look at it now." Joshua said, "Let me see that bread." It was moldy and smelled bad. The Scripture says, "The men of Israel examined their bread, but they did not consult the Lord." It looked as though the Gibeonites were telling the truth. Everything on the surface seemed as though they were straight-up people. So Joshua signed a peace treaty with them and said, "Fine, we give you our word. You can live here. We won't hurt you."

Three days later, the truth came out. Joshua found out they weren't who they said they were. They lived in neighboring cities. The Israelites were ready to let them have it, to wipe them out. But Joshua said, "No, don't touch them. We gave our word. If we break our agreement, God will come against us." It was a big headache that could have been avoided. The whole problem was that they did not consult the Lord. They just looked at what they saw on the surface. It looked as though the Gibeonites had traveled a great distance. They

> *God can see things we can't see. That's why you need to go to Him.*

seemed worn out and tired. It all made sense. But God can see things we can't see. That's why you need to go to Him before you get involved with people, before you sign that contract, before you put the money down. Do yourself a favor and consult with the Lord. People are not always who they say they are. They may show you one side, the side they want you to see, but God sees the whole package. You can't get so caught up in how fine someone looks. "Joel, he's tall, dark, handsome, and rich. I don't have to consult the Lord. The Lord just answered my prayer." You better step back or you may have somebody living with you who's not what you think.

Everything Is Not What It Seems

I heard about two young ladies who were in their early twenties and living in California. They had spent the day Christmas shopping in Tijuana, Mexico. When they returned to their car, one of the girls noticed what seemed to be a little dog that looked just like a Chihuahua. It was squirming on the ground near the gutter and was obviously in pain. Feeling sorry for it, she picked it up and put it in the trunk of their car. They were going to take it home and didn't want the border control to see it. One of the girls took it to her apartment and gave it some milk to try to nurse it back to health. She tried feeding it, but it wouldn't eat. She wrapped it up in a blanket and put it in the bed next to her, making sure it was okay through the night. The next morning it was doing even worse. She rushed it to the animal clinic, handed it to the veterinarian, and began to describe its symptoms. The doctor stopped her and said, "Where did you get this animal?" She was afraid that she would get in trouble for bringing it across the border, but she finally said, "My friend and I found this little Chihuahua in a gutter in Tijuana." He said, "Young lady, this is no Chihuahua. This is a Mexican river rat." What's my point? Everything is not what it seems. You'd better consult the Lord. You don't want any rats living in your house. Hopefully you're not thinking that it's already too late for you.

I'm asking you to go to God for daily direction. You're not going to make the best decisions if you're not consulting with God. Don't do as Joshua did and try to figure it out on your own. Do as David did and inquire of the Lord. Get up every morning and say, "God, what is it that You want me to do? Show me my assignment." When you come to God in humility, showing your dependence on Him, God will help navigate you through life. Are you taking time for your daily bread? Remember, you can't live off yesterday's manna. What worked in the past may not work today. Stay open for something

> *Stay open for something new.*

new. If you develop this habit of going to God for fresh manna, I believe and declare that God is going to lead you down the best path for your life. He's going to protect you from making mistakes, open the right doors, and bring the right people. It's heading your way.

CHAPTER THREE

Keep Speaking Victory

Our words are setting the direction for our lives. If you want to know what you're going to be like five years from now, listen to what you're saying about yourself today. "I'll never get well. I'll never break this addiction. I'll never meet the right person." You are prophesying your future. You can't speak defeat and have victory. You can't talk sickness and have health. You can't speak lack and struggle and have abundance. The Scripture says, "You will eat the fruit of your words." Pay attention to what you're saying about yourself, your family, your finances,

> *Pay attention to what you're saying about yourself, your family, your finances, and your health. You're going to become what you're continually saying.*

and your health. You're going to become what you're continually saying. That's why it's so important to get in a habit of speaking victory over your life. All through the day, you have to be saying, "I am blessed. I am strong. I am healthy. I am surrounded by favor. Something good is going to happen to me." The fruit of those words is blessings, favor, and abundance. It's not enough to just think it; we give life to our faith by speaking it out.

When you're in tough times, you can complain, talk about the problem, and say, "I can't believe this happened." Or you can say, "Father, thank You that You're fighting my battles. Thank You that what was meant for harm, You're turning to my advantage. Thank You that You always cause me to triumph, that I'll come out of this better than I was before." That's prophesying victory, that's prophesying a breakthrough. Don't use your words to describe the situation; use your words to change the situation. When you say, "I'll never get out of this problem," you're inviting defeat. When you say, "I'm not that talented," you're inviting limitations.

> *Don't use your words to describe the situation; use your words to change the situation.*

When you say, "I'll never accomplish my dreams. I don't have the connections," you're inviting mediocrity. You need to send out some new invitations. If you are struggling with depression, your report should be, "This is only temporary. This is not who I am. I am free, I am happy, and I have a bright future." "The dream may look too big, but I know that with God all things are possible. New doors are about to open. Good breaks are looking for me. The right people, divine connections, are headed my way."

The apostle Paul says in Ephesians, "Let everything you say be good and helpful, so that your words will be an encouragement to those who hear them." One person who hears your words is you. They go out of your mouth and back into your own ears. If you hear them long enough, they'll take root in your spirit. You believe what you say about yourself more than what anyone else says. There's nothing more powerful than you speaking victory over your own life.

> *You believe what you say about yourself more than what anyone else says.*

When my father went to be with the Lord and I stepped up to pastor the church, every thought told me that I couldn't minister. *Joel, you don't have the*

experience. You're not qualified. You're not that talented.
One thing I've learned is not to verbalize the negative. Don't give those thoughts life by speaking them
out. Instead of talking about how I felt—insecure,
unqualified, intimidated—I said what God said about
me. "I can do all things through Christ. I am strong in
the Lord. I am equipped, empowered, and anointed."
The whole time I was saying that, I didn't feel confident or qualified. I felt just the opposite, but as I kept
speaking victory, as I kept calling myself who God
says I am, it took root inside. Over time, I started
to feel strong, confident, and well able. I started to
see favor, new doors opening, and God taking me
where I never imagined. What happened? I ate the
fruit of my words. It may not happen overnight. You
have to keep speaking victory. Keep calling yourself
healthy. Keep declaring that your children are mighty
in the land. Keep declaring that your dreams are
coming to pass.

You Control the Rudder

In James 3, the tongue is compared to a rudder of a
ship. "Although a ship is large and driven by strong

winds, it is steered by a very small rudder wherever the pilot wants it to go." It's the same way with the tongue. Even though it's a small part of the body, it's steering your life. What you're saying is determining the direction you go. The good news is, you have control over the rudder. You control your tongue. Are you sending your words out in the direction you want your life to go? "I don't think I'm going to get well. The medical report doesn't look good." That's the wrong direction. Why don't you say what God says about you? "God is restoring health to me. By His stripes I am healed. I will live and not die." Are you saying, "My child has been off course so long. I

> *Are you sending your words out in the direction you want your life to go?*

don't think he'll ever make good decisions"? Change your rudder. You're headed the wrong way. You have to say, "Father, thank You that my children are mighty in the land. You say the seed of the righteous, my seed, is blessed. As for me and my house, we will serve the Lord." When you're talking defeat, "I don't see how I can get ahead, Joel. Nobody in my family has been successful, and this crisis is going to put my business under," you're headed toward defeat. When you talk failure, lack, and mediocrity, you're headed that way.

"I'm praying that God will help me." He will help you, but you control the rudder. You're setting the direction with your words. Are you in agreement with God? He says you are blessed. Are you saying something else? He says you are fearfully and wonderfully made, a masterpiece, crowned with favor. Are you calling yourself inferior, weak, not attractive? Start declaring what He promised. "Father, You say even in famine, the righteous will have more than enough. You say what I put my hands to will prosper and succeed." When someone asks how you're doing, don't go into all your troubles and how bad it is. Keep your ship going in the right direction. "I'm blessed. I'm strong. I'm valuable. I'm favored."

Think about a ship that's carrying very valuable cargo, such as oil, minerals, or equipment. All that valuable cargo is at the mercy of the small rudder of the ship. If the captain doesn't steer the ship the proper way, if the rudder isn't in the right position, the ship will never make it to the intended destination, and all that cargo will go to waste. In the same way, you are carrying valuable cargo. When God breathed His life into you, He put gifts, talents, and potential. You have seeds of greatness. You are destined to leave your mark, to take your family to a new level. The question is not, Are you equipped, are you favored, do you have what it takes? Your ship is fully loaded. The question is, Are you

> *Are you going to keep your rudder positioned in the right direction?*

going to keep your rudder positioned in the right direction? Are you going to speak victory, abundance, and new levels? Or are you going to talk as though you're average. "I can't get ahead. I never get any good breaks. This addiction has been in my family for years." You're not being limited by your circumstances; you're being limited by your words. Your rudder is positioned in the wrong direction. What you speak is what you're moving toward. When you speak victory, you're moving toward victory. When you speak health, you're moving toward health. When you speak overflow, more than enough, you're moving toward abundance.

Here's the key: You have to speak it before you see it. This is what faith is all about. The Scripture says, "Let the weak say, 'I am strong.'" You may not feel strong, but when you say, "I am strong," you're moving toward strength. You may be fighting an illness, but when you say, "I am healthy," you're moving toward health. Perhaps you feel stuck in your career, and it seems as though you've reached your limits, but you have to say, "New doors are about to open. Something good is going to happen to me. God is taking me from glory to glory." Then you're moving toward new levels, favor, something that you've never seen. Are you steering your ship in the direction you want your life to go? Is your rudder, your tongue, taking you to blessing, increase, and abundance? Or are you talking about what's not working out, or how you don't feel that talented, or that the obstacles are too big? That's going to keep you from your destiny.

Say Not

In the Scripture, God told Jeremiah that he was going to become a great prophet and speak to nations. But Jeremiah was young and afraid. The first thing he said was, "God, I can't speak to the nations. I'm too young. I wouldn't know what to say." God could have said, "Jeremiah, I understand. This seems over your head, but don't worry. I'm going to help you." No, God said, "Jeremiah, say not that you're too young." God told him to zip it up. He knew that if Jeremiah kept speaking those negative words, telling himself that he was too young, not qualified, and didn't have what it takes, he would never become who he was created to be. Your tongue is the rudder for your life. It's determining the direc-

> *The next time you're tempted to say something negative about yourself, your future, your children, or your finances, zip it up.*

tion. The next time you're tempted to say something negative about yourself, your future, your children, or your finances, zip it up. Don't steer yourself toward defeat. Say not that you're too young. Say not that you can't get well. Say not that you'll never meet the right person. Say not that you can't accomplish your dreams. God wouldn't have given them to you if you weren't well able.

After God told Jeremiah to not be afraid, it says, "The Lord reached out His hand and touched Jeremiah's lips and said, 'I have put my words in your mouth.'" God was saying, in effect, "Jeremiah, say what I say about you." Don't say how you feel, don't say what the experts say, and don't say what it looks like. Start saying what God says about you. It says in the book of Psalms, "He will crown the year with a bountiful harvest; even the hard pathways will overflow with abundance." You can go around saying, "This is such a tough year. I can't wait till it's over." Or you can say, "Father, thank You that even in hard times I will have more than enough. Thank You that You're an overflow God, that You're not limited by the circumstances, that You're not limited by the economy. Lord, thank You that I'm blessed in a down year, I'm favored in a famine, and I'm prosperous in a pandemic. I overflow. I have more than enough joy, more than enough strength, more than enough health." That's steering your ship toward increase, steering your ship toward overflow.

I talked with a young lady who was very successful in her career, but when the pandemic hit, things started to slow down. She was concerned about how it was going to work out. When she heard me talking about how it was going to be an overflow year, how the economy is not our source, but God is our source, something came alive inside. She started saying, "Lord, thank You that the economy is not my source, but You are my source. Thank You for an overflow year," and she kept repeating it under her breath, again and again, all through the day. It looked just the opposite. Things were going down, steadily decreasing, yet she was declaring increase, declaring favor, and talking about the greatness of our God. What was she doing? Steering her ship in the right direction. In difficult times, it's easy to talk about the problem, to complain, to be negative. That's when you have to dig down deep and say, "No, I'm going to keep speaking victory. God, You're my provider. You're my healer. You're my way maker. I may not see how it can happen, but I know that You're still in control."

She and her husband decided to start their own business. Against all odds, it took off, more than they ever imagined. They were able to close on their first house, and their business continues to increase. She said to me, "In the midst of all this uncertainty, with people afraid and struggling, we've seen favor in ways we never dreamed." That's what the Scripture says: "Even in hard times, the righteous will have more than enough." I don't think this would have happened if she had gone around negative and complaining. Pay attention to which way you're steering your ship.

> *When you're always bragging on the greatness of our God, talking about what He can do, declaring what He promised, you're going to draw in blessings, favor, and increase.*

What you're constantly talking about, you're drawing in. When you're always bragging on the greatness of our God, talking about what He can do, declaring what He promised, you're going to draw in blessings, favor, and increase.

Keep Speaking What God Says

Psalm 35 says, "Let them continually say, 'Let the Lord be magnified, who delights and takes pleasure in the prosperity of His children." It's interesting that they were supposed to say this continually. You would think they could say it once or twice and that would be enough. But there's something powerful when you go through the day not talking about how big the problem is, or how your back will probably never stop hurting, or how you don't see how your child is going to turn around. Instead, you're saying, "Let God be magnified who takes pleasure in prospering me, who takes pleasure in healing me, who takes pleasure in favoring me."

Are you taking time to declare God's goodness over your life? Are you speaking victory over your future? It's not enough to do it every once in a while. It needs to become a habit. All through the day we need to be declaring that we're blessed, we're strong, and we're healthy. When you wake up in the morning, say, "Lord, thank You for

> *Nothing happens until you speak. Your words give life to your faith.*

another beautiful day, and thank You that something good is going to happen to me today. Thank You that favor is surrounding me, blessings are chasing me down, angels are watching over me, and that Your being for me is more than the world being against me." That's setting your rudder in the right direction. You can't be silent and reach your potential. Nothing happens until you speak. Your words give life to your faith.

When Joshua was about to lead the Israelites into the Promised Land, God said to him, "This Book of the Law, these promises, shall not depart out of your mouth. You shall meditate on them day and night, so that you may be careful to do them. Then you will prosper and have good success." It doesn't say they shouldn't depart out of your mind. It doesn't say that if you think positive, you'll be fine. It doesn't say that if you read it enough. It says they should not depart out of your mouth. If you keep speaking what God says about you, you will have good success.

In Mark 5, there was a lady who had been sick for twelve years. She had spent all her money going to different doctors, but still nothing had helped. One day she heard that Jesus was passing through town. The Scripture says, "She kept saying to herself, 'When I get to Jesus, I will be made whole.'" In the midst of the sickness, she was prophesying health. Not just one time, but all through the day, she kept saying over and over, "Healing is coming, restoration is coming, a breakthrough is coming." When she saw Jesus, a crowd of people was packed in all around Him. She could have been discouraged and complained, but instead she kept saying, "This is my time. Things are about to change in my favor." As she kept speaking it, she got closer and closer. She finally reached out and touched Jesus' robe, and she was healed instantly. Notice the principle: Whatever you're constantly saying, you're moving toward.

> *Whatever you're constantly saying, you're moving toward.*

If you're always saying, "I'll never get out of debt," you're moving toward struggle and lack. If you're saying, "My marriage is not going to last. We don't get along," you're moving toward separation, toward a breakup. If you're saying, "I'll never get well. This sickness will be the end of me," you're moving toward defeat and mediocrity. But if you send your words out in a different direction, your life will go in a different direction. When you say, "I am blessed," you're moving toward blessing. When you say, "I have the favor of God," you're moving toward increase. When you say, "I'm excited about my future. Something good is going to happen to me," you are moving toward new opportunities and divine connections. When you say, "I'm going to break this addiction. I'm not going to live bound by this alcohol, by this anger, by this bad habit," you are moving toward freedom, breakthroughs, and victory. Pay attention to what you're saying. Your life is going in that direction.

See Yourself in a New Way

God gave Abram the promise that his wife, Sarai, would have a child, and he would be the father of a great nation. The problem was that they were both way too old. Abram was seventy-five years old. Sarai was barren, had never been able to have children, and had already gone through the change of life.

Sometimes God will give you a promise that seems impossible. You're too young or too old, or you don't have the connections, or the medical report is not good. You don't have to figure out how it's going to happen. Just get in agreement with God. "Father, You say that I'm going to have a baby, so thank You that my baby is on the way." The mistake we make too often is to send our words out in the wrong direction. "I can't have a baby. I can't get well. I'll never start my business." Negative words can stop what God has for you.

God told the Israelites that they would live in the Promised Land, the land flowing with milk and honey, but negative words kept them from going in. Ten of the twelve spies sent into the land came back and said, "The people are too big. There are giants in the land." The opposition didn't defeat them; their negative words defeated them. They said, "We're not able. We don't have what it takes." They became what they said. They prophesied their future. They turned away from the Promised Land and wandered in the desert for forty years. When God puts something in your heart, don't start talking about how it's

> *They became what they said.*

not going to happen, about what you don't have, or about how big the opposition is.

Abram was still waiting for his promised son at the age of ninety-nine. He had this promise that seemed impossible. God did something interesting. He changed his name from Abram to Abraham, which means "the father of many nations." He didn't feel like a father, but every time someone said, "Hello, Abraham," they were saying, "Hello, father of many nations." He could have thought, *They have the wrong person. I don't have any children.* When he met someone new, he would say, "Hello, I am Abraham." He was saying, "I am the father of many nations." He said that over and over, month after month, and it began to get down in his spirit. He had to see himself in a new way before the promise could come to pass. The way God changed his self-image was through his words. That's why it's so important, all through the day, under your breath, to be saying, "I'm blessed. I'm healthy. I'm strong. I'm successful. I'm talented. I'm attractive." That's helping to determine how you see yourself.

God also changed Sarai's name to Sarah, which means "princess." She didn't feel like a princess. She was barren. Women in that day who didn't have children were looked down on. She could have felt

> *Every time Abraham and Sarah said their names, their rudder was pointed toward the promise.*

inferior and ashamed, but when someone said, "Hello, Sarah," they were saying, "Hello, Princess." "Good morning, Sarah. Good morning, Princess." When she told people her name, she was saying, in effect, "I'm chosen. I'm favored. I'm blessed." She said all this while she was still barren. Your tongue is the rudder; it's deciding which direction your life is going to go. Every time Abraham and Sarah said their names, their rudder was pointed toward the promise. They kept declaring it, over and over. When Sarah was ninety years old, she gave birth to a son. God did the impossible.

What are you saying about your dreams, your finances, your children? "I'm too old. I've made too many mistakes. I don't have the talent." That's going to keep you from giving birth. You can't speak defeat and reach your potential. Why don't you start saying what God says about you? He calls you what you are before it happens, as He did with Abraham and Sarah. "But I don't feel blessed, healthy, or favored." That's okay, just get in agreement with God. He'll make things happen that you couldn't make happen.

Eat the Fruit of Your Words

I talked with a young man who came from a small town in Mississippi. He had a scholarship to play soccer at a major university, but his dream was to play football. During his junior year, he talked to the coaches about it, and they allowed him to switch from soccer to be a kicker on the football team. He was thrilled to be on the team, but the coaches never gave him a chance. For two years, he sat on the bench and never kicked a single field goal. At the end of his final college season, there was a scout day, when coaches come from professional teams and watch different players work out so they can evaluate them. He was hoping he would get some good leads, but none of the coaches were interested in him. It looked as though his days of playing football were over.

Driving home from college, he turned the radio on and came across our SiriusXM channel. He heard me talking about how a shift is coming, how you're just one phone call away from your destiny, how one touch of God's favor can catapult you to the next level. When he heard that, something ignited in his spirit. He knew this message was for him. When he got home, he used his cell phone to make a three-minute video telling people that he was going to play that year in the NFL. Most people thought he had lost his mind. He'd never kicked one field goal, had no track record, and he was saying he would be playing professional football. People told him that didn't make sense. He let that go in one ear and out the other, and he started speaking victory. "Father, thank You that opportunity is coming my way. Thank You that favor is causing me to stand out." He was setting his rudder in the right direction, prophesying his future.

Four hours after he made the video, he received a phone call from the kicking coach of the Cincinnati Bengals football team, inviting him to try out for the team. He couldn't believe it. He had never spoken to or met the coach. He went to the training camp, tried out, and against all odds, he made the team. He became the only African American football kicker in the NFL at that time. When you speak victory over your life, God will open doors that no person can shut. He'll take you where you can't go on your own. It's not enough to just believe the dreams He's put in your heart, the promises you're standing on. That's important, but something happens when you speak. Angels go to work, forces of darkness are broken, and good breaks come looking for you. When you're up against what seems permanent, just keep speaking victory. When the medical report is not good, keep

> *I'm talking about a lifestyle where you develop the habit of speaking health, speaking favor, speaking abundance.*

speaking health. When business is slow, keep speaking abundance. When the addiction seems like it will never change, keep speaking freedom. When your family member is off course, keep speaking breakthroughs. You keep declaring what God promised. You don't just try this for three days and then say it didn't work. I'm talking about a lifestyle where you develop the habit of speaking health, speaking favor, speaking abundance. When you do this continually, God says you will have good success.

You're going to eat the fruit of your words. Make sure that you're sending out words you want to eat. If it's not positive, hopeful, and faith-filled, zip it up. Say not that you can't get well; our God is a healer. Say not that you can't accomplish your dream; our God is a way maker. Say not that you'll never have enough; our God is a provider. Now get in agreement with Him. Start sending your words out in

> *You're going to eat the fruit of your words. Make sure that you're sending out words you want to eat.*

the right direction. If you keep speaking victory, as with the football player, I believe and declare good breaks are coming. As with the sick woman, healing is coming. As with Abraham, promises that seem impossible are about to come to pass. Problems that look permanent are about to turn around. Favor is coming, breakthroughs, restoration, and abundance.

CHAPTER FOUR

The Secret to Solving Problems

We all face challenges and things we're believing will turn around—a child who's off course, a sickness we're dealing with, a dream that seems impossible. We're praying, believing, and declaring God's promises, but nothing is changing. Sometimes God won't allow you to solve your own problem. The secret is that you have to help someone else solve their problem. You have to take the focus off yourself and be good to others in your time of need. As you sow that seed, that's what's going to bring the harvest you're waiting for. You'll be tempted to think, *I can't help someone else. I have my own challenges. I need to spend my energy trying to fix my situation.* If you take your hands off your problem and be good to someone else, God will put His hands on your problem and make things happen that you couldn't make happen. While you're working on their situation, you're not losing time, because God is working on your situation.

A friend of mine struggled with his relationship with his teenage son for many years. It was as though they were on different wavelengths. He tried his best to be loving, kind, and understanding, but they just couldn't get along. Everything was so contentious. Invariably, they would end up in an argument. He had prayed about it, quoted Scripture, asked God to help, but nothing improved in the relationship. Meanwhile, he was the coach of the neighborhood baseball team. There was a young man on the team who came from a single-parent home and was struggling with his schoolwork. When this father learned about this situation, he took the teen under his wing. He started bringing the young man home from baseball practice with his son, and he would help him with his homework. He tutored him, mentored him, and became a father figure in his life. This teenager admired him and looked up to him in a great way. About six months after the father started pouring into this young man, his relationship with his son began to improve. They got closer and started spending more time together. Today, they're the best of friends. You can't keep them apart.

The secret to solving his problem wasn't in praying more or in working harder. It was in helping someone else solve their problem. The Scripture says, "When Job prayed for his friends, his healing quickly came." How many times do you think that Job prayed for himself when he was dealing with his own sickness, enduring the pain week after week? To pray, "God, please restore health to me. Please free me from this pain," is good. That's releasing your faith. I'm simply saying to not stop there, because there are times when your break-through is tied to helping

> *There are times when your breakthrough is tied to helping someone else get their breakthrough.*

someone else get their breakthrough. Maybe you've been praying diligently, standing in faith so strong, but nothing is changing. Now it's time to go be a blessing. Look around for a need you can meet. Go pray for your neighbor who's under the weather, go encourage your coworker who's struggling, go help your friend accomplish her dream. As you're helping others, you can't see it, but God is helping you. He's lining up the healing, the breakthrough, the promotion for you. You can't sow a seed without reaping a harvest.

Help Solve Someone Else's Problem

When I was a young boy, Lakewood met in an auditorium that held a thousand people. The church was growing, and we needed to expand the building. My father asked the members of the congregation to be praying about what they could give toward the project. He was believing that the money would come in. At the time, there was a small Spanish-speaking church about six blocks from Lakewood. This church had already started construction on a small auditorium that would hold about a hundred people. My father noticed that their construction had stopped, and for several months nobody was working at the site. He had never met the pastor and didn't know anyone there, but one afternoon he decided to stop there and talk with some people. They told him that after they started the building, they ran into complications, and the project was more expensive than they had planned for. Now they had run out of finances to finish, and the project was stalled indefinitely.

My father was believing to raise the funds we needed to expand Lakewood. But my father told the congregation that instead of giving money to our building, he was going to take up an offering for their building. The congregation at Lakewood gave them enough money to finish their sanctuary. In the natural, that didn't make sense. We had a problem. We needed the funds to build our own sanctuary. But my father understood this principle: If you help someone else solve their problem, God will help solve your problem. Sometimes it doesn't make sense. But Proverbs 11 says, "It is possible to give away and have more; it is also possible to hold on too tightly and lose everything." God's ways are not our ways. Everything in you will say, "Focus on getting out of my problem and accomplishing my dream. I don't have time to help anyone else. Once I get this problem solved, I'll help others." But helping others is what's going to cause that problem to

> *"It is possible to give away and have more; it is also possible to hold on too tightly and lose everything."*

turn around. Giving your time, energy, and resources is what's going to open the windows of Heaven and cause your dreams to come to pass.

You would have thought that giving away those funds would have kept us from building our new church, but it was just the opposite. The funds came in for the foundation, and we paid it off. The funds came in for the steel, and we paid it off. The funds came in for the walls, the chairs, and the sound system, and we paid those off. The building was built debt-free. There were no delays and no complications. That was true not just for that building, but over the years my father built building after building, expansion after expansion, and paid cash every time. There was never a lack of finances or resources. I believe it all started when he helped the Spanish church with their problem. When he needed finances, when he had a challenge, he didn't just pray about it and believe. He helped solve someone else's problem.

When you make sacrifices to help other people's dreams come to pass, God will help make your dream come to pass. Don't live focused only on yourself— your problems, your sickness, your trouble at work. Get your mind off yourself and go be a blessing. Sow a seed. It doesn't have to be finances. You can sow encouragement. Go visit your loved one in the hospital. Call your friend and speak faith into their dreams. Make an extra plate of food for dinner and take it

> *When you make sacrifices to help other people's dreams come to pass, God will help make your dream come to pass.*

to your elderly neighbor. The Scripture says, "When it's in your power to do good, do not withhold it from others." That means when you know you can be a blessing, when you have the resources to help a person in need or you can teach them the skills you've learned, don't put it off. When you help solve their problem, you're not just being good to them, you're setting a miracle in motion for yourself. When you show favor, the Scripture says you will see favor.

Here's the beauty of it: When you help others, what you give is going to come back to you not in the same proportion, but pressed down and running over. My father helped the Spanish church one time, but in the years to come the blessings of that obedience kept coming.

> *When you help others, what you give is going to come back to you not in the same proportion, but pressed down and running over.*

When you're in difficulties, more than ever you need to look for opportunities to do good. When your dream seems impossible, find somebody you can help to make their dream come to pass. It's good to pray, believe, and work hard, but some things are not going to happen if you're just focused on yourself. As you bless others, God will bless you. As you show favor, favor will come to you. As you help solve their problem, God will solve your problem.

Seeds of Generosity Keep Producing

On the last Sunday that we had services at our old location before we moved into the Compaq Center, I left the service and was driving down the road that final time, feeling so grateful for all the things God had done. My mind was flooded with good memories and overwhelmed with where God was taking us. I looked up and there was a beautiful rainbow in the sky, as if God was smiling down on us and saying, "This chapter is over, and another great one is beginning." In a couple of minutes, I passed the little Spanish church that my father and Lakewood had helped some twenty-five years earlier. On their small outdoor sign, it said, "Thank you, Lakewood, for giving us our building."

My mind flashed back to that time when I was a little boy. I wondered if we would be going to the Compaq Center if my father had not helped that congregation in their time of need. Would I be seeing the blessing, the favor, the growth? My father could have thought, *I have my own problems. We have big challenges. We need a lot more money than they do.* But he didn't withhold the good when he had the opportunity. Much of this comes down to trusting God. "God, I need somebody to help me. I don't want to help them. I need these resources. I can't give them what I'm counting on." When you give your time, your talent, and your resources to help others in their time of need, you're never going to end up with less. That seed you're sowing is going to keep coming back to you. I'm reaping a harvest today from seeds of obedience that my mother and father sowed forty years ago. When you live a life of generosity, when you make sacrifices

> *That seed you're sowing is going to keep coming back to you.*

to help other people rise higher, it's not just going to affect you. It's going to affect your children. Those seeds keep on producing.

In 2 Kings 19, King Hezekiah was on the throne in Judah. He was one of David's descendants. The Assyrian army had surrounded the people of Judah and were about to attack. They were much bigger and stronger. Hezekiah didn't stand a chance. But when he prayed and asked God to help them, he received a message from the prophet Isaiah that the Assyrian army would not enter Jerusalem or even shoot their arrows into the city. God said they would return home in defeat. That very night an angel of the Lord destroyed 185,000 of the enemy army. The rest of the army turned around and went home just as God said. Hezekiah was so thrilled, so grateful. I can imagine he wondered why God was so good to him and why he had received such favor.

God's answer to Hezekiah was, "It is for the sake of my servant David that I have defended you." This took place nearly three hundred years after David died, yet David's legacy of seeds of obedience, seeds of helping others, and seeds of honoring God were still producing fruit in his family line. Every time you help someone in need, it's not only going to help you, but

you're storing up bless-
ings for your children.
Every time you solve
someone else's problem,
when you go the extra
mile and make sacrifices

> *Every time you help someone in need, you're storing up blessings for your children.*

for them to go further, you're sowing a seed not only
for you to go further, but for those who come after
you in your family line to go further. They will see
favor and protection because you made decisions that
honor God.

The Donkeys Are Coming

In the Scripture, Joseph had a big problem. When he
was a teenager, God put a dream in his heart that
he would be in leadership and do great things. But
his brothers were jealous of him. They didn't like
his big dream, so they threw him into a pit. They
were going to tell their father that he was killed by
a wild animal, but they ended up selling him into
slavery. Joseph was taken to Egypt where he worked
for a man named Potiphar, and he was eventually
put in charge of Potiphar's household. Even though

Joseph had a big problem, even though his dreams had been shattered, what did he do? Did he sit around in self-pity, blaming God and saying, "It's not fair"? No, in the midst of his problem, he helped Potiphar with his problem. He ran Potiphar's whole household, organized all the staff, made sure the grounds were clean, the property was secure, and the supplies were in place. Instead of just focusing on his problem, he was being good to someone else.

At one point, Joseph was falsely accused of a crime and put in prison. You would think that surely then he'd be bitter and discouraged. But in the prison, two of his cellmates had a problem. On the same night, each of the men had a dream and didn't understand what their dreams meant. Joseph didn't say, "Too bad for you. I'm depressed, I don't like you, and I don't like being here." He said, "I can interpret dreams. Let me help you with your problem." He interpreted their dreams correctly, and one of those cellmates got out of prison and was restored to his position of chief cupbearer to Pharaoh. Two years later, Pharaoh had two troubling dreams on the same night, and he didn't know what they meant. The cupbearer, Joseph's former cellmate, said, "I know someone who can interpret dreams." Joseph was brought into the palace and he told Pharaoh that the dreams had to do with the food supply, that there were seven years of famine coming, and they had seven years to store up grain and get everything in place for the drought. Pharaoh said, "There's no better person to do this than you, Joseph. You're the right man." Joseph was made second-in-charge of Egypt.

What was Joseph doing for Pharaoh? Solving a problem. He was being strategic, getting everything set up, using his expertise, his skills, and his talents to help the people who were holding him captive. He was so excellent at what he did that other nations came to study his operation and how he did things. I'm sure Joseph was grateful to be out of prison and to have this influential position, but he still missed his family. He never thought he would see his father, whom he loved so much, again. He'd already accepted that it was too late. But as he was being good to someone, helping Pharaoh with his problems, back home in Canaan, his brothers were loading up their donkeys and about to head to Egypt to try to purchase food. They had heard that the only

> *While Joseph was working on Pharaoh's problem, God was working on Joseph's problem.*

source of grain was at the Egyptian palace where Joseph was in charge. Notice what was happening. While Joseph was working on Pharaoh's problem, God was working on Joseph's problem. Joseph couldn't see it. Everything seemed the same, but what he didn't know was the donkeys were coming. His brothers were on the way.

I can imagine one evening there was a knock on the palace gates. The guards looked outside and there were all these shepherds and donkeys. The guards asked what they wanted, and they said they had come to buy grain. One of the guards went to Joseph and said, "We have some people who just arrived. They want to purchase grain." It was late in the day, and Joseph was tired. He was about to say, "Tell them to leave. I don't want to be bothered," but for some reason he changed his mind and went to meet them. He couldn't believe that these were his brothers. You would think he would want to get revenge. The truth was that he was so grateful to see them that he was overwhelmed with emotion. They didn't recognize him, but he eventually told them who he was, and they all wept. He asked if their father was still alive, and they said he was.

All those years when Joseph was helping other

people with their problems, doing the right thing even though it wasn't fair, God was watching the whole time. God sees your faithfulness. He sees you helping others when you need help, encouraging your friend when you need encouragement, praying for your neighbor who's not well when you're fighting an illness of your own. It may seem like nothing is happening, but God is working. You can't see it, but the donkeys are being loaded up. What you thought would never happen is on the way.

Joseph's father and entire family came to live with Joseph in Egypt. His father thought Joseph was dead, and Joseph thought his father had passed, but now the two of them were embracing and weeping. It was a dream come true. Joseph's problem was finally solved. It didn't happen the way he thought. He didn't go back to Canaan, but his family came to him. And they were all able to enjoy the favor and honor that God had given Joseph.

None of this would have happened if Joseph had been focused only on himself. "I have my own problems. I'm not going to help this man Potiphar. He needs to help me. I'm here unfairly. I'm not going to help this prisoner. He's never done anything for me. I'm not going to interpret Pharaoh's dream or use my talent to run the food supply. They need to do something for me." Joseph understood this principle: While you're helping other people solve their problems, God is working on your problems. You may think you can never get well, never break the addiction, never accomplish the dream. It's been too long. But if you do as Joseph did and keep being good to people, keep helping them solve their problems, keep helping their dreams come to pass, what you can't see is the donkeys are coming.

Do Yourself a Favor

What God started in your life, He's going to finish. He's going to surprise you. There's going to be a knock at the door, something you weren't expecting. It will be like when those brothers showed up at the palace. Healing is going to show up unexpectedly, freedom from that addiction. Suddenly, the right person comes looking for you, the opportunity opens up. You thought it was too late, but that whole time you were helping others, the donkeys were en route. God has not forgotten about you. Those seeds you've sown have not gone unnoticed. He sees those times you've come to church and served in the children's ministry or sang in the choir while you have

> *Those seeds you've sown have not gone unnoticed.*

challenges at home. You went out and prayed for others when you were dealing with an illness. You could have stayed home and thought, *God, when You do something for me, then I'll be my best.* You just kept being your best, being good to people, making sacrifices to help others, giving away what you needed for your dreams. Get ready for some surprises. Get ready for God to show out in your life. Get ready for something you didn't see coming. It's going to be unusual, uncommon. It's going to thrust you to a new level.

When I worked behind the scenes doing the television production for my father for seventeen years, my goal was to make him look the best that I could. I didn't have a lot of experience when I started, but I found the best lighting consultants, the best camera people. During the first year, we hired an older gentleman who had been the producer for the *Today* show. As he trained me on how to put the program together, I tried to be with him every minute. I spent hours working on the lighting, trying to make it better, and making sure the stage looked the best that it possibly could. At one point we decided to remodel the platform area. We had some very talented designers to help us. We were making a new podium as well, so I had them mock up a temporary podium that we could use to check the size and see how it fit my father. He came and stood behind it while we looked at it on camera and made a couple of adjustments. I wanted it to fit him just right. I wanted the stage area to be as perfect as it could be, so my father would look good. We finished the remodel, and it looked beautiful on camera. I was so proud, and it made my father shine.

A year later, my father went to be with the Lord. I never dreamed that one day I would be standing behind that podium. I never thought that I would be the one on that beautiful platform. I thought I was building it for my father, but I was really building it for me. When you're helping other people, you think you're doing them a favor, but you're really doing yourself a favor. As you help someone else shine, God is going to make sure that you shine. But sometimes we think, *I'm not going to help them succeed. That's going to make me*

> *As you help someone else shine, God is going to make sure that you shine.*

look less-than. I'm not going to give them my ideas and cause them to look better. I need to keep that for my own dreams. It's just the opposite. As you help others rise higher, God is going to help you rise higher. You're sowing a seed for where you want to go.

What You Can't See

My friends Rob and Laura Koke pastor a church in Austin, Texas. In 2009, their sixteen-year-old son Caleb was killed in an automobile accident. It was very hard, but they didn't get bitter. They didn't give up on life. They kept moving forward. Eventually, they started a charity in his name called the Caleb Foundation. They've built orphanages, hospitals, schools, and have done great work all over the world. At one of the three Caleb's House orphanages in Haiti, there were some young men who grew up there and graduated from high school. They decided to bring a few of the young men to Austin to intern at their church. One of those men noticed Rob and Laura's daughter, Danielle. They started dating and ended up falling in love. A few years ago, Danielle married this young man named Fred, who grew up in the orphanage the

Kokes started. All this was birthed out of the loss of their son.

What if Rob and Laura hadn't reached out to help others in their time of need? They could have lived sour, blaming God. "We're not going to help someone else. We need people to help us. We've been through loss and pain. We need someone to keep us encouraged." Instead their attitude was, *Yes, we're hurting. Yes, it's unfair. But God, we know when we help others, You'll help us. When we work on others' problems, You'll work on our problem.* They started sowing these seeds, taking care of the orphans, providing an education to the less fortunate, being good to people without expecting anything in return. They never dreamed when they started that orphanage that their son-in-law would grow up there. They never dreamed that young man would be the one their daughter would fall in love with and that he would become a part of their family. When you help others, you think you're just being good to them. You don't know what God is up to. You can't be good to somebody else without God being good back to you. You don't know the favor and the blessings that are connected to your helping someone else rise higher.

I wonder what we miss when we stay focused on ourselves, when we focus only on what we've lost, how we've been hurt and have problems, and are saying, "God, You have to help me." Go be a blessing. Your miracle is waiting for you as you help others. Sometimes the whole reason you can't solve your own problems is because what you need is found in solving someone else's problem. As with Joseph and the donkeys, when you help other people succeed, something you thought you would never see again is coming. As with Rob

> *Your miracle is waiting for you as you help others.*

and Laura, your son-in-law is coming, something you weren't expecting. As with my father, new sanctuaries are coming, the resources to fulfill your dreams. While you're helping others, what you can't see is God is helping you. Things are happening behind the scenes.

Maybe you have been doing this already. You've been going out of your way to be a blessing, making sacrifices to be good to others, spending your time helping a friend with their problem. Get ready. The donkeys are coming. What you're believing for is already en route. I believe and declare that those seeds you're sowing are about to come back to you pressed down, shaken together, and running over. It's going to be more than you imagined—more healing, more breakthroughs, more favor.

CHAPTER FIVE

No More Distractions

The older we get, the more we realize that we're not going to be here forever. Life is flying by. It seems like just the other day I was in high school, and now that my own children have graduated from college, I think, *Where has the time gone?* When you realize how fast time is going, it should bring a sense of urgency, a sense of focus. Your assignment has an expiration date. Your time on this Earth is not unlimited. When the time came for Jesus to be crucified, the Scripture says, "When the hour had come, He set His face toward Jerusalem." There came a time when there was no more going to the desert and feeding five thousand, no more waiting at the well for the Samaritan woman, no more stopping by Zacchaeus's house for dinner. Those things were good for that season, but now Jesus didn't have time for distractions from His main purpose. His hour had come. God is saying to you, "Your hour has come." If you're going to reach your highest potential, you have to do as Jesus did and set your face. You can't get distracted by things that are keeping you from your purpose.

You don't have time to waste being worried about what people think about you. Your time is too valuable for you to respond to every critic and every negative comment, to try to convince people that you really are okay. That's a distraction. Everyone is not going to like you; everyone is not going to accept you. Quit wasting time trying to convince someone to understand

> *Quit wasting time trying to convince someone to understand you who's determined to misunderstand you.*

you who's determined to misunderstand you. They don't want to be for you, and that's okay. Don't get bitter about it. You don't need them to fulfill your destiny. The enemy would love for you to spend your time and energy trying to win over someone who's never going to be won over. If you change and do everything they want, they will still find some reason to not like you. Set your face and run your race.

The people you need to be for you will be for you. God has already lined up people who will celebrate you, people who will stick with you, people who see the best in you.

Keep Your Face Set

Too often we're trying to convince people to be our friends and to spend time with us. If someone doesn't see the gift that you are, if they don't recognize your talents and value your friendship, do yourself a favor and move on. No offense to them, but they're not a part of your destiny. You don't have to play up to people and let them manipulate you. You don't have to hope they call you and include you in their group. The people God has for you don't have to be talked into liking you. You won't be able to keep them away. They'll light up when you walk in the room. They can't wait to spend time with you. They'll go out of their way to do you favors. Don't spend another minute trying to convince someone to call you, to come see you, to spend time with you. If you have to talk them into it, they're not for you. They're a distraction.

"Well, these people at work are saying negative things about me. They're trying to make me look bad." It's not your job to straighten them out. Let God fight your battles. Let God be your vindicator. You're not supposed to engage in every conflict. Don't fight battles that are not between you and your destiny. Most of the things we face are simply distractions. You have to stay focused and exercise discipline. You have to say, "I'm not going to respond. I'm not going to sink down to their level and waste my time and energy. I have a destiny to fulfill. My hour has come." Proverbs 20 says, "Avoiding a fight is a mark of honor." It's easy to get in conflict, to get offended, upset, and want to pay people back. That doesn't take any discipline. Avoiding a fight, not taking the bait, and not being drawn into the conflict take your face being set. When something comes against you, you need to ask yourself, "Is this a battle worth fighting, or is it simply a distraction?"

> *"Avoiding a fight is a mark of honor."*

A person cuts you off in traffic. Is that worth getting upset and spending your emotional energy over, when you're never going to see that person again? The coworker who leaves you out and doesn't give you any credit on a project. Do you think he can keep you from your destiny? Do you think that somehow he's more powerful than what God has ordained for you? He's a distraction. The only way he can hinder you is if you get baited into the conflict. The best thing you can do is ignore it. Don't give it the time of day. Keep your face set. Keep honoring God, being your best. He'll get you to where you're supposed to be.

Is It a Battle Worth Fighting?

When David saw Goliath taunting the Israelite army, he asked what the reward was for killing the giant. He didn't just run out and try to fight Goliath because he was saying bad things and belittling the Israelites. Sure, David didn't like it and it annoyed him, but he didn't get involved in battles that weren't between him and his destiny. David was told that whoever killed Goliath would get the king's daughter for his wife and his family would be exempt from taxes. With this one victory, David's whole family line could change. He would go from a low-income family of shepherds to royalty. He would be in the king's family. David thought, *This is a battle worth engaging. This is something worth spending my time and energy on. It stands between me and my destiny.* I'm not saying to be passive and don't fight any battles, but I'm saying to look at what the spoils are. Will it just feed your ego, where you pay them back and make them look bad? Or will it propel you into your destiny?

We fight too many battles that don't matter. "Well, they're talking about me. I'm going to set them straight." But when you get them fixed, somebody else will start talking. Here's what I've learned—nobody talks about people who aren't doing anything. Nobody tries to discredit someone who has no influence. Take it as a compliment. The reason they're talking is because you're a difference maker, you're a world changer. They can see your influence, your gifts, and the favor on your life. The brighter the light, the more the heat. The higher you go, the more people can see you. Sometimes instead of celebrating you, people will get jealous, try to pull you down, and get

> *Sometimes instead of celebrating you, people will get jealous, try to pull you down, and get you into conflict.*

you into conflict. Don't take the bait. It's a distraction. Keep your face set. Stay focused on your goals.

Before David fought Goliath, his father had asked him to take a provision of food to his three brothers who were soldiers out on the battlefield. David gave the food to his oldest brother, Eliab, who was jealous of David. He said in front of some of the other soldiers, "David, what are you doing here, and what have you done with those few sheep you were supposed to be taking care of?" Instead of thanking David for traveling for days to bring them food, he insulted David, tried to belittle him. Now David had killed a lion and a bear with his own hands in the shepherds' fields. He might have been small, but I'm sure he could have taken care of his brother. It would have been no problem for David to show everyone how tough he was. But David thought, *What are the spoils? What good is it going to do me if I embarrass my brother in front of his peers like he did me?* He realized all that would do was feed his ego. There was no reward. The Scripture says that David turned and walked away. He ignored Eliab's insults. One reason we're talking about David is that he knew what battles to fight. He didn't engage in every conflict.

When Someone Does Not Want Peace

The apostle Paul says in Romans 12, "As far as you can, live at peace with every person." It doesn't say that you're always going to be at peace with everyone. Some people don't want to have peace with you. David's brother didn't want peace. Eliab was jealous and small-minded. He wanted to stir things up. David had to accept that his brother wasn't going to be at peace with him. "Joel, shouldn't I go the extra mile? Shouldn't I be the bigger person?" Yes, but if you do all that and others still don't want to have peace, you need to move on. You have a destiny to fulfill. Your assignment is waiting on you. You can't worry about people who don't want to have peace with you. I'm all for being nice, but at some point you have to put your foot down and say, "You may have a problem with me, but I don't have time to have a problem with you. I don't mean any disrespect, but I don't have time to play petty games and try to convince you that I'm okay." Life is too short for you to try to have peace with people

> *You can't worry about people who don't want to have peace with you.*

who don't want to have peace with you. You may have some relatives you love, but you have to love them from a distance. Don't frustrate yourself trying to make something happen that they don't want. That's not being disrespectful; that's being responsible with the gifts God has given you.

My nature is to be a peacemaker. I want everyone to be happy. I'll go the extra mile four hundred times to make peace. But some people have their own issues. They don't get along with themselves, so how are they going to get along with you? They don't like who they are, so how are they going to like who you are? No matter what you do, it's not going to be enough. They're going to find fault, to be critical, to try to make you feel guilty. If you keep trying to appease them, keep bending over backward, spending all your time and energy trying to keep them happy, all that's doing is letting them control you. Be nice, but don't get distracted trying to make peace with someone who doesn't really want peace. We all have people in our life who are like David's brother. They don't like seeing you happy, going places, rising higher. It's not about you; it's about the favor on your life, it's about the blessing God put on you. Don't take it personally. Keep your face set.

You won't fulfill your destiny trying to keep everyone happy. Some people who make the most withdrawals from your life put in the least deposits. They're high maintenance people. They expect you to always be there to help them, to encourage them, to meet every demand, but when you need them, they're never around. They're too busy. If that friendship is one-sided, where they're doing all the taking and none of the giving, you need to make a change. I've heard it said that you should quit swimming across

> *You weren't created to be controlled by others, to not be able to pursue your dreams and have time to do what God put in your heart.*

an ocean to be good to someone who won't jump across a puddle to be good to you. If they get offended because you can't meet every expectation, they aren't a true friend. They just want you for what you can do for them. Those people are distractions. You need to gradually break away from people who are like that. You weren't created to be controlled by others, to not be able to pursue your dreams and have time to do what God put in your heart. "Joel, what if they get upset? What if they get their feelings hurt?" I would rather disappoint a few people than disappoint God. When you come to the end of life, you're not going to give an account to people of what you did with your time, your talents, and your resources. You're going to give an account to God.

Come Out from Under a False Debt

Romans 13 says, "Owe no person anything except to love them." The only thing you really owe people is to love them. That does not include going around with a false sense of responsibility, thinking you have to keep everyone happy, letting people put their demands on you, making you feel like you're carrying a debt. "I have to keep you fixed, keep you cheered up. I have to call you every day or you'll get upset. I have to make sure I play up to you or you won't be my friend." That's carrying a debt that you don't owe. Always be respectful, but don't go through life trying to please everyone. If you try to keep everyone happy, the one person who won't be happy is you. Come out from under that debt. Be kind, go the extra mile, but don't be a people pleaser.

As I was growing up, this was hard for me to learn

> *It's very freeing when you realize you're not responsible for keeping other people happy.*

because I wanted people to like me. I would go out of my way, do anything for people. I finally learned what I'm telling you, that no matter how much you do, no matter how good you are, some people are going to find fault with you, and it's not going to be enough. It's very freeing when you realize you're not responsible for keeping other people happy. You're responsible for keeping yourself happy. I don't mean you should live selfishly and think only of yourself, but don't take on the false sense of responsibility thinking other people's happiness depends on you.

In Chapter Two, I wrote about the friends I went out of my way to help. If this couple ever needed anything, I was always available. I would call and check on them. But the feeling I got from them, even after I gave them money to help with their move to another city, was that I was never doing enough. They were never satisfied and always had a complaint. They were constantly finding fault, trying to make me feel guilty. I was so concerned that they were going to get upset and weren't going to like me.

Then one day it dawned on me that they never made any deposits in my life; they only made withdrawals. I was nice, but I quit letting them control me. When I stopped, you would have thought that I'd taken their firstborn child. They tried to make me feel guilty and ashamed. I thought, *I love you, but I don't owe you anything else.*

Freedom from People

If people are controlling you, it's not their fault; it's yours. You have to make a change. This is your hour. You can't reach your destiny dragging people along, feeling responsible for keeping everyone happy. Your time is too valuable for you to go around trying to figure out how you can please everyone. I know people who spend more time being worried about what people think about them than they do focusing on their own dreams, their own goals. It's great to get free from addictions, free from depression, free from sickness, but one of

> *If people are controlling you, it's not their fault; it's yours.*

the greatest freedoms is when you get free from people. Everyone has their own opinions, and these days it's easier than ever to express them. In just a few seconds on social media, people can tell you what they think about you, what you should wear, how you should raise your children, how you should spend your money, and what you're doing wrong. People who can't even run their own lives are quick to tell you how to run yours.

It's good to receive advice and to listen to wise counsel, but nobody can hear what you hear inside. Other people may mean well, but they don't know what God put in you. They don't know the dreams, the desires, or the calling inside. You have to be bold to follow what's in your heart. You can't worry about what other people are going to think. *What if they don't agree? What if they get offended?* If someone gets upset because you won't take their advice, that's their problem. If you live by the opinions of others, you'll never become who you were created to be, because people will try to keep you in their box, in what they think you should be.

It's like this grandfather I heard about who took his small grandson to town on a donkey. He started off letting his grandson ride the donkey, and he was walking alongside of him. Someone passed by and said, "Look at that selfish boy making that old man walk." The grandfather heard it and lifted the boy off the donkey, and he rode the donkey with his grandson walking by his side. Someone came along and said, "Look at that man making that little boy walk while he rides." Hearing that, the grandfather pulled the little boy up, and they both rode the donkey. In a few minutes, another person said, "How cruel of the two of you to place such a heavy load on the donkey." By the time they got to town, the grandfather and grandson were carrying the donkey.

Everyone has a right to have their opinion, and you have the right not to take it. No matter what you do, some people are not going to understand. Are you carrying the donkey, pressured into being what people want you to be, not wanting to disappoint anyone? It's time to put that donkey down. Start running your race. Follow what God put in your heart.

> *Everyone has a right to have their opinion, and you have the right not to take it.*

Don't Be Squeezed into Someone's Mold

When my father went to be with the Lord and I stepped up to pastor in 1999, I had a lot of people give me advice. They told me how to run the church, how I should minister, and what direction we should go. One very prominent minister we had known for a long time called and told me what I should do. I respect him and his opinions, but nothing he told me bore witness inside. I felt pressured to be what he wanted me to be, and I felt pressured to be what others wanted me to be. These were all good opinions from good people, but deep down I knew what direction I was supposed to go. I didn't know how it would turn out, but I thought, *I'm not going to be squeezed into someone else's mold.* When I told the prominent minister that what he shared with me was not what was in my heart, he thought I was making a mistake. He didn't agree. But I knew when I came to the end, he wouldn't be on the throne. I wouldn't have to answer to him. I did what was in my heart, and God has taken me further than I've ever dreamed.

Don't let somebody squeeze you into their mold.

God is doing a new thing. He's going to take you further than your parents, further than those who have gone before

> *Don't let somebody squeeze you into their mold. God is doing a new thing.*

you. Listen to their advice, but be strong and follow that still small voice inside. Nobody can hear God's direction for your life as you can. God doesn't give someone else more insight about your destiny than He does you. Others may see things, but God speaks to your spirit. Sometimes people won't understand you. They don't like it when you break out of the box. Someone said to me, "Joel, I like the old days. You've forgotten where you've come from." I thought, *I haven't forgotten. I just don't want to stay there.* God is a progressive God. Don't get stuck in tradition, in what was. *What are they going to think? What if they don't accept me? What if they don't approve me?* You don't need their approval. The Most High God has approved you. The One who breathed life into you has accepted you.

You have to set your face. This is your hour. There is greatness in you. God is calling you out of the ordinary, out of what was, out of what you're used to. He has things in your future that are going

> *God is calling you out of the ordinary, out of what was, out of what you're used to.*

to break barriers. You're going to go where no one in your family has gone. It's going to be unusual, uncommon. Everyone is not going to understand, and some people will find fault with you, try to discredit you, and will think you're missing it. That's okay. No one who's ever done anything great has done it without opposition, without critics, without people thinking they were off course. Keep your face set.

Don't Be a People Pleaser

My father always said that he would never move Lakewood from the original location. When I became the pastor, I wasn't about to move it either. I was young and new. I wasn't going to rock the boat. But we needed a bigger place, and when we looked for land around the area, it didn't work out. Then the Compaq Center became available, and it was about twenty minutes from the original location. I knew it was supposed to be ours. I felt it so strongly in my spirit, but I didn't know what the church members would think. For all those years, they had heard my father say he wouldn't move it. Thoughts whispered, *This is not right. People are not going to understand. You'd better stay in the box.* I felt one thing in my spirit, but my mind was telling me the opposite. One day I heard something down inside say, "Your father said he would never move it, but I never said that you wouldn't move." That was all I needed. I announced that we were going to pursue the Compaq Center.

Nearly 100 percent of the people were for it, but one man came up who was all bent out of shape. "Joel, your father said he would never move the church. This is not right. You're making a mistake. If you move it, I'm not going to come." Some people won't accept the new thing God has put in your heart. They're stuck in what was, when God is telling you what is. It's much bigger. It's a new level. It's greater influence. It's uncommon favor. It's something that you've never seen. Don't let the fear of what people are going to think keep you in your box.

> They're stuck in what was, when God is telling you what is.

This is one reason King Saul lost the throne. God told him to do certain things, which he did only partially. When the prophet Samuel confronted him, Saul said, "I disobeyed the Lord's instructions because I was afraid of the people, so I did what they asked." Saul knew the right thing to do. God had put greatness in him, and He was going to take him to amazing places, but Saul didn't want to disappoint the people. He didn't want to rock the boat. You can't be a people pleaser and reach your potential. People will try to squeeze you into what they're used to, into what they think. Take advice, listen to counsel, but you may have to disappoint a few people in order to reach your destiny.

Quit Being Afraid of People

In Genesis 12, God told Abraham to leave his country, his relatives, and his father's house and go to the land of Canaan. Abraham gathered his belongings, his flocks and herds, but when he left, he took along his nephew Lot. God had just told him to leave his relatives. Maybe he thought Lot would be offended, that it would hurt his feelings. Abraham knew the right thing to do, but he was afraid someone might not understand. When they arrived in Canaan, the land couldn't sustain both he and Lot and all their flocks and herds. Their shepherds started arguing, which led to strife and division. It was because Lot wasn't supposed to be there in the first place. Finally, Lot moved to a different part of the country. The Scripture says, "After Lot left, God spoke to Abraham and said, 'Look around. All the land you can see I will give to you.'"

It's interesting that God didn't speak until after Lot left. When Abraham finally did what he knew he was supposed to do and Lot moved away, Abraham stepped into the blessing. Do you have some Lots in your life? Are you letting the fear of what people will think hold you back? *What if they get upset? What if we move the church? What if they don't understand me?* Is that keeping you from hearing the new thing

> *Do you have some Lots in your life?*

God has for you? Why don't you get rid of Lot? Quit being afraid of people. Quit letting them squeeze you into their mold. Don't get stuck in tradition, in what was. God has blessings that you haven't seen. He has increase that you haven't imagined.

Now do your part and get rid of the distractions. No more living to please people. No more living worried about what others think. No more fighting battles that don't matter. This is your hour. It's time to get focused. It's time to set your face. If you do this, I believe and declare, as with Abraham, you're about to see favor in unprecedented ways, new doors about to open, divine connections, healing, and breakthroughs.

CHAPTER SIX

Ready to Rise

We all face things in life that try to push us down. It's easy to lose our passion and think that's the way it's always going to be. But God didn't create you to be overcome, He created you as an overcomer. He's put something in your spirit called "bounce-back." Bounce-back means that when you get knocked down, you don't stay down. There is a force breathing in your direction, making things happen that you couldn't make happen, giving you strength that you didn't have. It causes you to rise up. Because you have bounce-back, that difficulty cannot defeat you. It may hold you back temporarily, but it's just a matter of

God didn't create you to be overcome, He created you as an overcomer.

time before you rise back up. You may have things that have come against you now. Thoughts will tell you, *You'll never get well. The pandemic ruined your finances. You'll always struggle with this addiction.* Don't believe those lies. You may be down, but that's not your final destination. God is saying, "Get ready to rise. Get ready for favor, get ready for breakthroughs, get ready for healing." What was meant for your harm, God is turning to your advantage.

The prophet Micah says, "Rejoice not over me, my enemy; when I fall, I will arise." He wasn't complaining about the trouble, and he wasn't discouraged over being knocked down, because he understood this principle that there was bounce-back in his spirit. In the middle of the difficulty, he was speaking victory. If you're going to come out of that challenge, you have to do as Micah did and say, "This problem didn't come to stay. It came to pass. God being for me is more than the world being against me. I shall arise." When you say that, forces of darkness tremble. When you declare "I shall arise," angels go to work. No more, "It's never going to change. My business is never going to make it. My child will never

> *When you declare "I shall arise," angels go to work.*

get back on course." Zip that up. If you talk defeat, you're going to have defeat. Say with Micah, "Yes, I've had difficulties. I'm not denying the problem, and I'm not acting as though it doesn't exist. All I'm saying is that I'm not staying here. I shall arise. I will see the goodness of God. My latter days will be better than my former days."

God hasn't brought you this far to leave you. He won't let you get in a problem that He can't get you out of. That person who walked out on you didn't stop your destiny. Quit giving them that much power, thinking that they ruined your life. God has somebody better coming. David says, "God lifted me out of a pit and set my feet on a rock." You may be in the pit, so to speak; you don't see how you can get out. The good news is that

> *God hasn't brought you this far to leave you. He won't let you get in a problem that He can't get you out of.*

you don't have to get out by yourself. The Most High God is about to lift you out. He's about to free you from that addiction. He's about to turn the medical report around. He's about to open new doors, bring new opportunities, and new relationships. That pit is not your destiny. Get ready to rise.

The apostle Paul says, "The same Spirit who raised Christ from the dead lives inside you." The forces of darkness did their best to stop Jesus, but they couldn't keep Him from rising. That tells me that nothing you face—no natural disaster, no sickness, no addiction, no lost dream—can keep you from your purpose. The enemy may have done his best, but his best will never be enough.

Bounce-Back Power

A few years ago we had a big hurricane in Houston. I noticed all the different kinds of trees that were blown down. Huge oak trees that were three or four feet around. I saw pine trees that were over a hundred feet tall lying in yard after yard. Big trees and small trees—none of them could withstand the hurricane-force winds. There was only one type of tree that wasn't blown down. It was the palm tree. It's because God designed the palm tree to withstand the storms. Unlike most other trees, the palm tree is able to bend so it doesn't break. A certain kind of palm tree can bend all the way over to where the top is almost touching the ground. During the hurricane, it may stay all bent over for three or four hours, looking as though it's done. But when the wind dies down, when the storm is over, it stands right back up to where it was before. All the other trees are still down on the ground. What's the difference? God put bounce-back in the palm tree. It may get pushed over, but it's only temporary.

Psalm 92 says, "The righteous will flourish like a palm tree." The reason God chose a palm tree and not an oak or pine tree is He knew we would go through storms. He knew things would try to push us down and keep us from our destiny, so He says, "I'm going to make you like a palm tree. I'm going to put bounce-back in your spirit." You may go through difficulties, a loss, or a disappointment, but at some point the winds will stop, the storm will pass, and like that palm tree, you'll come right back up. You may be bent over now. You're facing challenges, and thoughts are telling you that it's never going to work out. Get ready to rise. You have bounce-back power. When that

> *You may go through difficulties, a loss, or a disappointment, but at some point the winds will stop, the storm will pass, and like that palm tree, you'll come right back up.*

storm is over, you're not going to be lying down, defeated and beat up. You're going to rise up healthy, blessed, and prosperous. You're not going to look like what you've been through. Nobody is going to be able to tell that you even had that difficulty. What I love about God is that He doesn't just bring you through the storm; He makes the enemy pay for bringing the trouble.

When the palm tree is bent over during the hurricane, you would think that's damaging the tree and making it weaker, but research shows just the opposite. When the tree is being pushed over and stretched by the winds, that's strengthening the root system and giving it new opportunities for growth. After the storm, when the palm tree straightens back up, it's actually stronger than it was before. When you come out of that storm, when you straighten back up, you're not going to be the same. You're going to be stronger, healthier, better off, and ready for new growth.

When you're in difficult times, you need to remind yourself, "I may bend, but I'm not going to break." God won't let you face anything that's too much for you to handle. Things may be coming against you, but being down is not your destiny. Defeat is not how your story ends. Sickness, trouble, and not having enough are not permanent. I believe even now the winds are starting to subside. Forces that have hindered you are being broken. Powers of darkness are being pushed back. You're about to see breakthroughs, freedom, joy, and victory.

Wait and See What Will Happen

The prophet Micah lists all the negative things that had happened to him. In Micah 7, he talked about how he was overwhelmed with sorrow and how he had gone through bad breaks. It is very depressing. If he had stopped there, we wouldn't be reading about him. But he went on to say, "But as for me, I'm not giving up. I'm sticking around to see what God will do. I know He will make things right." He had an attitude of faith that says, "I've come too far to stop now." He was expecting God to turn it around. That's why he could say to his enemies, "Don't rejoice when I fall. I shall arise."

Sometimes we've been in the storm for so long that we've forgotten what it's like to be standing up. The enemy would love to convince us to settle for being bent over—living in dysfunction, bitter over who hurt us, thinking that we'll never be happy again. We need to do as Micah did and say, "Yes, I've had some bad breaks. Yes, life has thrown me some curves.

> *The enemy would love to convince us to settle for being bent over—living in dysfunction, bitter over who hurt us, thinking that we'll never be happy again.*

But I'm not giving up on my dreams. I'm not settling for mediocrity. I'm sticking around to see what God is up to. I know He's going to make things right." Don't get talked out of your dreams. Don't let the delays, the unfair childhood, or the unexpected storms convince you that you've seen your best days. God is up to something. What looks like a setback is all a part of His plan. He may not have sent the difficulty, but He wouldn't allow it if it was going to keep you from your destiny. If you have this attitude of faith, God will make things right in your life. He'll restore what the enemy tried to steal. He'll pay you back for the wrongs. He'll open doors that you couldn't open. He will get you to your destiny.

Keep an Attitude of Faith

I mentioned earlier that in Genesis 37, when Joseph was a teenager, God gave him a dream that he would be in leadership and have great influence. He had ten older brothers, but he was the favorite son of their father, Jacob. Because Joseph was born later in Jacob's life, Jacob treated him differently. He even had a special robe of many colors made for Joseph. I'm sure that Joseph was proud of that robe. It made him stand out and gave him prestige. His brothers were jealous of Joseph. They didn't like the special treatment he received, and they didn't like the fact that he had these dreams, that he thought he was going to do something great. One day his father asked Joseph to travel to another city to check on his brothers who were feeding their flocks. When they saw Joseph coming from a distance, wearing the colorful robe, they agreed that this was their big chance to kill him. But one of the brothers persuaded the rest of them to just take Joseph's robe and throw him into a pit. They were going to put blood on the robe and tell their father he had been eaten by a wild animal.

About that time, a caravan of Ishmaelites came passing by. The brothers decided to sell Joseph as a slave instead of leaving him in the pit to die. It's interesting how God will always have the right people show up at the right time. That caravan had been traveling for months. They had left their homes long before Joseph went to check on his brothers, but God has everything figured out. He knows what you're going to need, when you're going to need it, and who's going to need to be there. You don't

> *He's not only in control of your life, He's in control of the circumstances around you.*

have to worry. God has it all lined up. He's going to get you to your destiny. People can't stop you, and neither can bad breaks or injustice. God is ordering your steps. He's not only in control of your life, He's in control of the circumstances around you.

Joseph went from being the favorite son, wearing the colorful robe, to being a slave in a foreign country, working for an Egyptian man named Potiphar. Year after year went by, and Joseph kept doing the right thing, being good to people who weren't being good to him. I can imagine that on many lonely nights he thought about home, about that robe he used to have and what it meant. Tears would fill his eyes. Thoughts would whisper, *It's not fair. You'll never accomplish your dream, you'll never see your father again, and you'll never have that robe of many colors.* But I can hear Joseph praying deep down, "Father, thank You that what You started in my life, You will finish. I don't see a way, but I know You have a way. I believe I will rise again. What You promised me will come to pass."

Thirteen years after Joseph was thrown into the pit, Pharaoh had a troubling dream and none of his magicians and wise men could interpret its meaning. Joseph was being held unjustly in prison, and one of his former cellmates remembered that he could interpret dreams. They brought Joseph into the palace, and he told Pharaoh how the dream had to do with the food supply and how they needed to store up grain and get everything prepared for the coming famine. Pharaoh was so impressed with Joseph. When his advisors discussed who should be appointed for the new position, Pharaoh told them, "No one can do it better than Joseph." He put Joseph in charge of the whole nation, saying, "No one will move hand or foot in all of Egypt without your approval." Pharaoh had his staff bring a royal robe for Joseph. He took off his prison clothes, took off his slave clothes, and put on a robe of honor, a robe of influence, a robe of authority.

Let Go of the Robe of Many Colors

Imagine now Joseph thinking back about the robe his brothers had taken from him, the robe that represented favor. He had been disappointed at the time. He wanted it back. It didn't seem fair, but now he realized that without losing the robe of many colors, he would never have had the robe of authority, the robe that said, "I'm in charge of a nation." If you knew what God has in store for you, you wouldn't be discouraged over the robe of many colors that was taken away—the job that didn't work out, the person who walked away, the loan that didn't go through. If you could see the robe of authority that's coming, the robe of influence, the robe of abundance, the robe of unprecedented favor, you wouldn't be bitter over who hurt you, upset over the time in the pit, or frustrated by what you

> *Your story doesn't end with a robe of many colors that you lost.*

lost. What God has in your future is so amazing that you'll never complain about your past. You may be down now, but as with Joseph, get ready to rise. Favor is coming like you've never seen. God is about to do something unusual, something uncommon, that will catapult you to a new level. Your story doesn't end with a robe of many colors that you lost. It doesn't end with a dream that didn't work out, a relationship that didn't make it, or a business that went down.

The robe of many colors was simply foreshadowing what God was about to do for Joseph. It was supposed to be temporary. It wasn't supposed to last. If the door closed, accept it and move on. Don't spend your life wishing you had the robe of many colors back when God has something so much better in your future. Don't go around bitter because someone threw you in a pit. God saw when someone betrayed you, someone cheated you in a business deal, or a dream didn't work out. He wouldn't have let them take the colorful robe, He wouldn't have let that bad break happen, if it were going to keep you from your destiny.

How many of us are longing for the robe of many colors? Wishing we could go back to when we knew we were favored, before the setback, before the health

You haven't seen, heard, or imagined where God is taking you.

issue, before the pandemic. Here's the key: Not having the robe of many colors doesn't mean you don't have favor; it means that greater favor is coming. You had to lose that robe to step into the awesome future God has in store. You haven't seen, heard, or imagined where God is taking you. If you feel as though you're in a pit, that's okay, because the pit is leading you to the palace. If you had a setback, that's okay, because it's setting you up for greater honor, greater influence, greater authority. Don't sit around sour, wishing for the robe of many colors. Get ready for the greater things that God is about to do.

Joseph was in charge of the food supply. There was a great famine in the land, and the only place that had grain was in Egypt. One day Joseph's brothers, the same ones who threw him into the pit, traveled from Canaan to the palace looking to purchase food. Joseph came out, but they didn't recognize him. The last time they had seen Joseph, he was in the pit, defeated, without a future, but God has the final say. They knew him in the pit, but now Joseph was so successful, had so much influence and prestige, that they didn't recognize him. That's the way God vindicates. When He raises you up, you'll be so blessed, so favored, that your enemies don't recognize you. Thirteen years earlier, Joseph was down, and his brothers were up. Joseph was in the pit, and they were on top. Now Joseph was up, and his brothers were down. Joseph was in charge, and his brothers were in need. When you let God fight your battles, there will be a day, as with Joseph, when the tables are turned. You will be up, and those who tried to stop you will be down. God knows how to make things right.

You may be in a tough time, but hang in there and see what God is up to. Keep believing, keep praying, and keep dreaming. Your time is coming. The pit is only temporary. The depression, the sickness, or the lack is not how your story ends. God is working behind the scenes. You are closer than you think. It's going to happen sooner than it looks. God is about to surprise you. Joseph woke up one morning in prison, and it seemed like another ordinary day. A few hours later, he was the prime

> *Joseph woke up one morning in prison, and it seemed like another ordinary day. A few hours later, he was the prime minister of Egypt.*

minister of Egypt. There wasn't any sign of it coming. That's the way God works. Many times you don't see anything happening and suddenly things fall into place—suddenly your health turns around, suddenly you meet the right person, suddenly you're promoted.

Let God Arise

The psalmist says, "Let God arise and His enemies be scattered." "Let" means you have to allow it, meaning in your thoughts. When you let God arise, you make Him bigger than your problems, bigger than the sickness, bigger than the financial trouble. You focus on His greatness. You think about His power. You talk about how He's brought you through in the past. You go around bragging on what He's done, declaring His promises. "No weapon formed against me will prosper. What was meant for my harm, God is turning to my advantage." The bigger you make God, the smaller your problems become, and the more faith will rise in your heart.

But the enemy is always trying to get us to let the problem arise. Maybe your child is off course. It's easy to talk about how he's not making good decisions, how he's never going to reach his destiny, and how you don't know what you did wrong. You're letting the wrong thing arise. Turn it around and start letting God arise. "Father, thank You that as for me and my house, we will serve the Lord. Thank You that my children will be mighty in the land. Thank You that my seed, the seed of the righteous, is blessed." That's letting God arise. That's what causes things to change. When you speak defeat, you bring defeat on the scene. But when you speak victory, you bring God on the scene. He created the universe. He flung stars into space. There's nothing that He can't do.

Maybe you're struggling in your finances, your business is slow, or you were laid off at work. You can either let that defeat arise and feel discouraged and worried, or you can let God arise. "Father, thank You that I will lend and not borrow. The economy is not my source; You are my source. You said You would prosper me even in a desert." When you let God arise, the Scripture says your enemies will be scattered. Depression, lack, and trouble cannot stand against our God. When you let Him arise, chains that have held you back are broken, problems that look permanent will turn around. When God arises, favor comes, new doors open, and things happen that you couldn't make happen.

Now the question is, Are you letting God arise or are you letting the problem arise? All through the day, it's so important to keep a song of praise in your heart. Instead of worrying, thinking about all the things that are wrong and what might not work

> *Are you letting God arise or are you letting the problem arise?*

out, in your thoughts you have to say, "Lord, thank You that there's nothing You can't do. There's not a mountain You can't move. You're a way maker, a promise keeper, a miracle worker." Take the same time that you would normally worry and turn it into worship. That's not just being positive, that's letting God arise. That's what allows the most powerful force in the universe to go to work on your behalf.

Get the Robe That Belongs to You

"Well, Joel, this all sounds good, but I don't think I'm going to rise back up. I've made a lot of mistakes. Nobody did me wrong like Joseph's brothers did. I brought the trouble on myself." Jesus told a story about a young man like this in Luke 15. He asked his father for his inheritance early, left home, and spent all the money partying, living wild, making poor decisions. When he ran out of funds, he got a job feeding hogs in a field. He was so desperate, so hungry, that he had to eat the hog food to survive. One day he was sitting around depressed, mad at himself, feeling condemned. He began to think about home and how even the servants at his father's house had a hot meal every day. They had plenty of food while he was out in the field starving. The Scripture says, "He came to himself and said, 'I will arise and go to my father's house.'" He made a decision that he wasn't going to stay in that defeat. He wasn't going to sit around depressed, feeling guilty, beating himself up. He was going home.

He didn't know how his father would respond. He didn't know if his father would tell him to stay off the property. But when the father saw him a long way off, he started running toward his son, hugged him and kissed him. The son was wearing the dirty, smelly clothes from the hog field. The first thing the father said was, "Go get the best robe and put it on my son." It was not just any robe, not one that had been used, not a hand-me-down. No, it was the finest robe. It's interesting that God gave Joseph a royal

> *The prodigal son had to make the decision that he wasn't going to sit around discouraged, defeated, and thinking about all the mistakes he had made.*

robe of influence, a robe of authority, and He gave this young man a robe of honor, a robe of favor. Both of them rose out of what was holding them back. The difference between the two is that God caused Joseph to rise up. He didn't have to do anything to make it happen. He just kept honoring God, being his best, and Pharaoh called him in. But the prodigal son had to make the decision that he wasn't going to sit around discouraged, defeated, and thinking about all the mistakes he had made. If he had not said, "I will arise," he would never have seen the coat of favor.

I'm wondering if you are waiting for God to do something for you when He's waiting for you to say, "I will arise. I'm not going to go through life beating myself up, living condemned. Yes, I've made mistakes, but I know I'm forgiven. I know I've been redeemed." If you will arise, there's a robe of favor waiting for you, a robe of honor. The mistakes you made didn't cancel your destiny. Quit listening to the accuser, reminding you of everything you've done wrong. God has already forgiven you. Now forgive yourself and move on. It's time to arise and go to your father's house. The Scripture says, "A good person falls seven times, but they rise again." Get

> *If you will arise, there's a robe of favor waiting for you, a robe of honor.*

your fire back. Get your passion back. Nothing you've done is too much for the mercy of God. He knew every mistake we would ever make. He's already taken into account our wrong turns. He has a plan even for the times when we've missed it. Now arise and go get that robe that belongs to you. You can still become who you were created to be.

When the winds blow in your life, when the storms come, remember this principle: There's bounce-back in your spirit. You may bend, but you're not going to break. Like the palm tree, you're going to come right back up. All through the day, let God arise in your thoughts. Keep thanking Him for His promises, making Him bigger than what you're facing. If you do this, I believe and declare that as with Joseph, you're going to see promotion, vindication, and break-throughs. God is going to make things happen that you didn't see coming. You may have lost the robe of many colors, but get ready for the robe of authority, the robe of influence, the robe of favor.

ACKNOWLEDGMENTS

In this book I offer many stories shared with me by friends, members of our congregation, and people I've met around the world. I appreciate and acknowledge their contributions and support. Some of those mentioned in the book are people I have not met personally, and in a few cases, we've changed the names to protect the privacy of individuals. I give honor to all those to whom honor is due. As the son of a church leader and a pastor myself, I've listened to countless sermons and presentations, so in some cases I can't remember the exact source of a story.

I am indebted to the amazing staff of Lakewood Church, the wonderful members of Lakewood who share their stories with me, and those around the world who generously support our ministry and make it possible to bring hope to a world in need. I am grateful to all those who follow our services on television, the

Internet, SiriusXM, and through the podcasts. You are all part of our Lakewood family.

I offer special thanks also to all the pastors across the country who are members of our Champions Network.

Once again, I am grateful for a wonderful team of professionals who helped me put this book together for you. Leading them is my FaithWords/Hachette publisher, Daisy Hutton, along with team members Patsy Jones, Billy Clark, and Karin Mathis. I truly appreciate the editorial contributions of wordsmith Lance Wubbels.

I am grateful also to my literary agents Jan Miller Rich and Shannon Marven at Dupree Miller & Associates.

And last but not least, thanks to my wife, Victoria, and our children, Jonathan and Alexandra, who are my sources of daily inspiration, as well as our closest family members, who serve as day-to-day leaders of our ministry, including my mother, Dodie; my brother, Paul, and his wife, Jennifer; my sister Lisa and her husband, Kevin; and my brother-in-law Don and his wife, Jackelyn.

We Want to Hear from You!

Each week, I close our international television broadcast by giving the audience an opportunity to make Jesus the Lord of their lives. I'd like to extend that same opportunity to you. Are you at peace with God? A void exists in every person's heart that only God can fill. I'm not talking about joining a church or finding religion. I'm talking about finding life and peace and happiness. Would you pray with me today? Just say, "Lord Jesus, I repent of my sins. I ask You to come into my heart. I make You my Lord and Savior."

Friend, if you prayed that simple prayer, I believe you have been "born again." I encourage you to attend a good Bible-based church and keep God in first place in your life. For free information on how you can grow stronger in your spiritual life, please feel free to contact us.

Victoria and I love you, and we'll be praying for you. We're believing for God's best for you, that you will see your dreams come to pass. We'd love to hear from you!

To contact us, write to:

Joel and Victoria Osteen
PO Box #4271
Houston, TX 77210

Or you can reach us online at www.joelosteen.com.

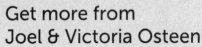